SCATTERED

Faith in Unfamiliar Times

Gene Brack

ISBN: 978-1-7348321-0-5 (Hardcover)
ISBN: 978-1-7348321-1-2 (Paperback)
ISBN: 978-1-7348321-2-9 (Kindle)
ISBN: 978-1-7348321-3-6 (Audiobook)

Cover Design by 100Covers.com
Interior Design by FormattedBooks.com

DEDICATION

This book is dedicated to my wife, JoAn, who has lived and learned the contents of this book with me through nearly 50 years of marriage.

It is also dedicated to our five amazing children:

Laura, Stephen, Charles, Michael, and PJ.

We live indebted to the Lord Jesus Christ for His word, grace, and faithfulness in our lives. We also live knowing this book's theme:

> *"God is passionately invested in us becoming someone we could never be without His direction and intervention."*
> GENE BRACK

TABLE OF CONTENTS

ACKNOWLEDGMENTS

Kelly Stickel and Scott Howard for their friendship and encouragement. Parents, Barney and Mae Brack, for raising me in a Christian home.

FOREWORD

It wasn't opportunity knocking, it was a transition rattling and handshaking its way into my life, uninvited. The invasion of that particular transition threatened everything familiar. My scattered memories of better times were left in the wake of it, fighting for legacy. Some transitions in life are like that, but not all. There's another variety of transitions. They're the kind that we initiate. What I've learned through both kinds is that all transitions matter. They matter because their ultimate purpose is transformation! I must never forget that. But, neither should you.

Those scattered by religious persecution 2,000 years ago struggled. Ultimately, their struggle forced them through transitional times that they didn't see coming. It changed them and they changed the world! James, half brother of Jesus, wrote them from Jerusalem's Church leadership in that first century. His letter is an eye-opening epistle of consequence relevant to all who have ever felt trapped in transitions, wanted or unwanted. Perhaps you've been there?

James' letter confronts a people that he labels 'scattered like seeds.' His words feel at first like a slap in their face but ultimately morphs into a life-giving salve. I've found that the paradigm shift that trying times offer is optional. The challenges are also optional. But the opportunities are temporary. So are the tests. Make note and hold on to my conclusion:

Transitions matter because they are transformational.

I've learned from James' letter that in all transitions **Opportunity** knocks, **Testing** comes daily and **Listening** has to be sharpened. I know, also, that listening is no more optional than asking for **Wisdom**. Most challenging is **Reaching Out** to help others in spite of our own personal chaos. But, just like the joy that comes in the morning, is the joy that seems to rise as we clarify our **Expectations** and lean into the **Grace** of God. Some of these seven factors take us quietly and some almost violently. But the finish line remains the same: Transition's ultimate purpose is always transformation. I believe firmly that **God is passionately invested in us becoming someone that we could never be, without His direction and intervention.**

This is transition's story, the prequel to transformation. I call it by its domestic name:

SCATTERED

GENE BRACK,
LIFE LONG LEARNER

INTRODUCTION

As followers of Jesus, we are in the constant flux of spiritual change.

As leaders, we juggle problem solving every day.

As parents, we balance the challenge of parenting with what we treasure as parents.

In crisis mode, we volley decisions that have life and death consequences.

For example, uprooting and relocating to an unfamiliar geographic location checks all the boxes marked 'stress'! So do ambitious enterprises of our own making. Regardless of their origin, all transitions have a tendency to scatter us. Scattered happens as we outgrow jobs, careers, or as those around us outgrow us! Complacency, boredom, and any sense of loss can scatter us mentally, spiritually, and emotionally. But there is always hope. Yes, but that hope is often compromised by a magnetic attraction to go back to our more familiar times.

In the unpredictable times of the first century, James, half-brother of Jesus, wrote a letter to believers being persecuted.

FOUNDATIONAL SCRIPTURE:

> *My fellow believers, when it seems as though you are facing nothing but difficulties, see it as an invaluable opportunity to experience the greatest joy that you can! For you know that when your faith is tested it stirs up power within you to endure all things. And then as your endurance grows even stronger it will release perfection into every part of your being until there is nothing missing and nothing lacking.*
>
> JAMES 1:2-4

HERE'S THE BREAKDOWN OF THIS SCRIPTURE:

- Seeing invaluable opportunities
- Experiencing the greatest joy
- Faith is always tested
- Testing stirs up power for endurance
- Endurance perfects (matures) us

James' letter confronted their faith. Scattered times confronts our faith, as well. We have to counter the challenge of scattered times with God's Word. Pulling truths from James' letter provides us with practical and scriptural applications. Leveraging these truths in the face of what's scattering us emotionally, mentally or spiritually carries the potential to change everything. These truths are not a sequence of steps. They are a collage of life-giving principles with the potential to stir up power within us.

THE SEVEN PRINCIPLES THAT GIVE US THE ADVANTAGE IN SCATTERED TIMES:

- **Opportunity**
- **Tests**
- **Listening**
- **Wisdom**
- **Reaching Out**
- **Expectations**
- **Grace**

These principles will define the chapters of the book. Some definitions you will need to know:

Scattered – *Disconnected or overwhelming challenges with emotional, physical, mental, or spiritual consequences. Examples include, but aren't limited to, uncomfortable or challenging transitions especially when what has always been familiar suddenly becomes unfamiliar. Such times happen due to changes in our geographic locations, career choices, relationships, finances, social standing, faith, or other norms.*

Leveraging – *Use (something) for maximum advantage. For example, leveraging the weight of something greater to offset something of a lesser weight.*

Bias – *An inclination of temperament or outlook. Bias in favor of or against an idea, talent, or strength.*

Opportunity – *A set of circumstances that makes it possible to do something, be something or to make a difference.*

Passion Bible Translation – *Unless otherwise noted, all scripture are from this translation.*

This book is about navigating through scattered times and seasons. As people of faith, we have to navigate life without losing our true identity and faith in Jesus Christ. That's the challenge. That's also the challenge the Apostle James wrote about in his letter to those scattered by persecution. Let me introduce you to Seven Truths that helped them see, seize, and navigate through their scattered times. They learned to leverage *Opportunity, Testing, Listening, Wisdom, Reaching Out, Expectations, and Grace.*

Like Jesus, they maneuvered through a sea of decisions and opportunities. It matters that we do the same. To some extent, His journey is everyone's journey. As He lived, so lived those who followed Him. If you're a believer, you're in the same race with the rest of us. If you're not a believer, there's still a race. I trust these Seven Truths will change your perspective on faith.

1

THE OPPORTUNITY PRINCIPLE: DECISIONS

In the middle of difficulty lies opportunity.
—*Albert Einstein*

Have you ever lived on the wrong side of history? James almost did. What gives him credibility is how he lived during scattered times. We can imagine what it was like growing up as Jesus' half-brother. Mary, Jesus' mother, believed Jesus to be the long, awaited Messiah. Her friends believed the same. They traveled with Jesus and experienced the miracles and heard his teaching. James and the disgruntled brothers rarely did. Their hearts kept their distance just in case He wasn't who He said He was. (John 7:5)

To Jesus' half-siblings, the things Jesus taught were controversial and embarrassing. His choice of words and ministry techniques left them embarrassed. Publicly, they kept a low profile but privately they were quick to get angry and speak out. They were slow to listen, indulging more in their traditional mindsets than processing the wisdom of their brother's teaching. Thus, during Jesus' three years of ministry, they lived on the wrong side of history.

The resurrection of Jesus awakened them. James leaned fully into the compelling revelation of who Jesus really was. The 40 days between the resurrection and Jesus' ascension were game changers in James' heart. He became a follower. He joined the 120 followers in the upper room and experienced the power of the Holy Spirit on the Day of Pentecost. He was all in! Peter's radical preaching that day added 3,000 followers to those who had already believed the Gospel. Thousands began following the apostles!

The increasing multitude of followers challenged the religious culture of the day. Compared to the miracle-working and anointed preaching of the disciples, the Jewish religious crowd were viewed as a powerless minority. They felt marginalized. As the Gospel continued to spread, the Jewish religious leaders resorted to radical maneuvers to literally kill the movement. Imprisonment and execution became their only hope for a resurgence of their political and religious power. Conflict reached a dramatic momentum when the religious sects managed to behead one of the original twelve. That's when persecution went into full swing. Believers scattered to other Roman territories, but James stayed behind in Jerusalem and quickly rose through the ranks of leadership.

When those scattered by persecution began to struggle with their faith in foreign cultures, James stepped in. It was his letter to them that realigned their congregation with the power of their faith. The Holy Spirit's wisdom mixed with James' earlier experience as an unbeliever stabilized the movement. The letter was shared from church to church. James' writing shifted the church forward. Their adherence to his principles reignited the scattered believers. Their faith at this intersection of Christianity changed them, and they change the world.

What about us? Difficulties in scattered and unfamiliar times test our faith. A careful read of James' letter highlights the strategies that stabilized the early church. In its simplicity, you will find the practical wisdom to regain your footing. The resurgence of their faith accelerated the movement of Christianity. The message of the Gospel spread.

In this chapter, you will find the resources you need to see the invaluable opportunities staring you in the face. The scriptural truths and experiences in this chapter will shift your focus from what has scattered you to what confirms you. As God's Word always does, you will engage the power of the Holy Spirit and move the trajectory of your life forward. Let's get started.

Scattered times have a tendency to throw us into rivers of opportunity without warning. Life may feel much like white water rafting at night on a river we've never navigated and with a boat load of people we've never met. Ready or not, the river is always moving. We have to redefine ourselves in its movement. The boat load of people may not be up for the challenge, but we have to be. This is the discovery aspect of every life-giving opportunity. Remember opportunity generates movement. Movement shakes things. Debris from our yesterdays may not make the cut. We can't carry everything up the mountain of opportunity. In fact, we often need new *everything*!

In unfamiliar seasons, we may feel like a moving target. We may feel under attack and vulnerable. Life-giving opportunity becomes like the brass ring. Grabbing it will require that we *suck the marrow** out of every life-giving option in front of us. (*Dead Poets Society reference intended. See the movie). It's our choice to ride out the opportunity. We have to do more than just see it. We have to explore it like a child with a new toy. More importantly, we have to see ourselves as the one needed to meet the challenge.

Unlike the scattered times of Christians persecuted 2,000 years ago, scattered times today may begin when life at work or home seems monotonous. We may find ourselves feeling detached from everything around us. Like living in a parallel universe, we are forced to navigate the waters of daily life. Yet, at the same time, we hunger for something more. Scattered times repeat themselves throughout our lives. We may feel inside like everything is becoming unfamiliar, even when nothing on the outside has changed. We learn to navigate such times without all our favorite and familiar props. At some point, you may view every opportunity as suspect. Or you may see options on every hand. It's like dating. We buddy up to multiple opportunities only to find they aren't the one. So, we keep searching, discovering, exploring. Life becomes unsettling. Hunger drives us.

If we refuse to change or dig in our heels, we'll stop the opportunity in midstream. Consequently, we'll find ourselves refusing to rethink the absolutes of our best practices. We may think that radical opportunity is not our forte. Maybe, mediocrity is us. Transitions in scattered times take us to critical intersections. Jumping ship is one of those intersections. Remember transitions matter. Their purpose is to bring us to a transformation. So, it's not just about the opportunity. It's really about the transitions that transform us into a better version of ourselves. This is the back and forth interplay that becomes our daily life.

THE 'WATER INTO WINE' MIRACLE

In John 4, Mary approaches her son's hand to do his first public miracle. Jesus doesn't seem to be budging. The setting is a wedding in Cana. The crisis? The wedding party has run out of wine. In the custom of the day, running out of wine at a wedding is a crisis. An unacceptable scenario is unwrapping. What was Jesus thinking? It was an opportunity. He knew that if He did this *water into wine miracle*, it would be His first public miracle. But He hesitated. Why? Good question. Here's the answer: He knew this one decision would be a definitive moment in His life. It was about more than wine. Jesus said to Mary, perhaps thinking out loud to Himself:

> *If I do this, it won't change anything for you, but it will change everything for me!*
>
> JOHN 2:4

He was right. That one miracle did change everything. It began with a decision. That decision defined Him. 'Miracle Worker' forever tagged His life and unfolded His purpose. With every miracle, Jesus took a step closer and closer to the crucifixion. Opportunity changed Him.

Decisions that change everything unfold a lifetime of opportunities. When the fear of change keeps us indecisive, we become defined by that fear. On the other hand, when we take on a life-giving opportunity, we grow. We connect. Our purpose unfolds. Everything changes.

Opportunity hinges on the power of a decision. After the resurrection of Christ many made the decision to follow Him. Their decision would not only define them, but it would change them. Religious persecution followed. They became scattered like seeds and sown among Gentile nations. Persecution pushed them into unfamiliar territories. Their faith was challenged.

Our decisions define us, especially in scattered times. The consequences of decision making tend to throw us a few curves along the way. But if we leverage opportunities, even in tough times, we grow. Our character matures. We're strengthened. Seeing scattered times as destructive, limits the richness of their opportunities. Decisions define us. Opportunities change us.

Seeing an opportunity is one thing. Seeing it clearly in its' ugliest form is another thing. Our initial perception of ourselves in an opportunity may be superficial, even naive. We have to look deeper into the mirror of an opportunity to see all its possibilities and complexities. If we don't, we'll see the transition as our enemy. We'll see ourselves as a victim. Seeing the ugly side of an opportunity brings us to another intersection. Do we continue or make a turn? What can we do with ugly? Good News: God's truth can trump seeing 'ugly'!

Take, for instance, when Jesus and the disciples got news from Bethany that their friend Lazarus was deathly ill. Mary and Martha, Lazarus' sisters, sent an urgent message that frantically communicated: 'drop everything and get yourself here quick'. But Jesus stayed put! His disciples were more than perplexed with His decision. They thought 'ugly'! Jesus thought opportunity. There is something in this story that offers us a critical life lesson for making decisions in unfamiliar times. What they didn't suspect was that for Jesus one phase of His life was timing out and another one was punching in!

By the time Jesus and the disciples traveled to Bethany, Lazarus was dead and buried. The town was grief-stricken. Mary and Martha wrestled with knowledge that if Jesus had arrived earlier, their brother would still be alive. Jesus wept. The key here is in how Jesus made His decision not to come earlier. If we miss it, we'll miss the process by which He made every decision.

What Jesus understood in that moment was that Lazarus had to die. Why? Because Jesus had to raise him from the dead. Why? Because Jesus was headed to the cross. And? In the aftermath of the resurrection of Lazarus, the crowd would divide between those who jeered at Jesus and those who cheered Him. Their divided opinions would get ugly. The jeers would hasten Jesus to the cross. In the larger Kingdom narrative where Jesus lived, the cross was already on the calendar. Jesus had to die. Why? So, He could rise from the dead. It was an intersection that stumped His followers, but the key to every decision Jesus made was this:

**Jesus always made decisions in the
context of the bigger picture.**

Like us, Jesus was stretched. He continually grew in wisdom. At this point in his life, He was in the home stretch. Like every decision He had made previously, this decision required that He make it in the context of the bigger picture. He lived His life focused on Kingdom business. He made the tough calls. Those calls time out our previous phase of life.

When opportunity stretches us or gets ugly, it is best to think in the context of the bigger picture. The poorer choice is to make decisions in the frustration and emotional heat of the moment. Seeing the initial opportunity is one thing, seeing its potential when life gets ugly is another thing. Transitions require it. Intersections are part of it.

CONTRIBUTORS VS CONSUMERS

One more important truth must be factored. We are on the planet as contributors in life, not merely as consumers. Being a consumer is easier because consuming is more familiar. Being a contributor can get crazy because more is expected of us. Life-giving decisions are viewed differently. As contributors, we march to a different drum. We allow opportunities to change what's trending in our hearts. We toughen up. We become more pliable and more vulnerable.

We make decisions that others might choke on. We process life differently. We make the tough calls.

Only as contributors do we tap into a personal toughness that pushes the limits of our responsibility and keeps us in the context of the bigger picture.

No toughness is gained by living engrained in what we've already done. As contributors, we push our limits. We go beyond the familiar understanding of ourselves. Consumers typically see themselves through a glass darkly. They look for opportunities that are 100% about themselves. But if we engage in life-giving opportunities, we begin to see ourselves as contributors. That means we see ourselves from God's perspective. At that level, decision-making changes our identity. This is when life-giving opportunities transform us. This whole contributor aspect is the plot within the plot of all transitions. Expect their encounter in scattered and unfamiliar times. You might need to re-read this paragraph to grasp its truth. I had to! Ask yourself: How do you see yourself. Contributor or Consumer? Ready? Let's move on.

SENSING WHAT'S VITAL

The Apostle Paul was a contributor.

> *And this I pray: that your love may abound yet more and more and extend to its fullest development in knowledge and all keen insight [that your love may display itself in greater depth of acquaintance and more comprehensive discernment].*
>
> *So that you may surely learn to sense what is vital, and approve and prize what is excellent and of real value*

[recognizing the highest and the best and distinguishing the moral differences], and that you may be untainted and pure and unerring and blameless [so that with hearts sincere and certain and unsullied, you may approach] the day of Christ [not stumbling nor causing others to stumble]
PHILIPPIANS 1:9-10 (AMPLIFIED BIBLE)

We may never discover who we really are unless we leave the familiar and abound in love for what's transitioning us. Seeing invaluable opportunity comes with a price. We have to allow our skillsets and mindsets to be stretched beyond our mental, emotional and spiritual comfort zones. The extension of God's love through us as contributors rather than as consumers requires stretching. **The key: discern what's vital & go for the stretch!** That's how God toughens us. We have to discern what's vital. It's our choice. Embrace the stretch.

Scattered times push us into unfamiliar territory. The unfamiliar is like a jungle. The people we find there may reject us and yet need us! They may keep their distance. But as we *discern what's vital* something wonderful happens inside of us. This *wonderful* may first seem threatening, but in time this *wonderful* brings a new identify. Our personal perspective of our life gets an update. We grow our perception of ourselves beyond the school yard norm of our past. We reevaluate relationships. When we sense what's vital for others, we see ourselves as contributors rather than as consumers. What we sense from God's point of view differs greatly from our previous viewpoints. Sensing what's vital changes everything.

In our new familiar, God pushes us to discover strengths we don't know we have. He wants to stir up His power beyond the ways we've always trusted Him. God is more than the Sunday School version we learned as kids. We have to toughen up. Why? Because as we toughen up, God's power rises within us. We live no more on the sidelines of life, but in the mainstream. We see needs and discover within us new strengths to meet them. We find our uniqueness in developing new strengths. Bulking up spiritually readies us for the next season of opportunities. Contributors are not closed minded. We don't limit opportunities to our comfort zones. We become pioneers. We explore. We toughen up.

Embracing spiritual toughness powers up God-given strengths for maximum capacity. Spiritual toughness leans expectantly into where God is taking us.

SEEING OPPORTUNITY THROUGH OUR PERSONAL BIAS*

*(*Bias may refer to something we favor or something we are against. In this context, bias refers to favoring strengths one has.)*

David's bias! Allow me to take you back thousands of years ago to a familiar story that altered a young man's universe. It's the familiar story of David as a young shepherd. You know his story but let me connect it to your story.

Goliath was viewed as an obstacle by King Saul and his merry men. But Goliath was viewed by David as an opportunity. David moved in his bias for action. Everyone has a bias. I have a bias for teaching, leadership, and creativity. I see every opportunity through my bias! So did David. He took action.

Saul and those around him moved in their bias for inaction. Their bias was formational posturing without action. That equates to maintenance without movement. For David, the stalemate that froze the Israelites' army presented circumstances favorable for his bias for action. He was made for this. David lived intentionally. He had proven himself to himself in isolation generated by His faith in God. He knew what it was to come to the table of the Lord in the presence of his enemies. Do you know how to come to the table of the Lord in the presence of your enemies? In the presence of your doubts? In the presence of what's scattering you? Digest that for a few moments.

Everyone has to prove themselves to themselves in hidden places. So, it was for David that in the shepherd's field, hidden from his family, he quietly changed. Turns out that the shepherd field isn't for wimps! Don't let a childhood understanding of Psalm 23 fool you. David was a warrior in the making. He toughened up in the shepherd's field to prepare for the battlefield.

All his life, David loved throwing stones. It was in his blood. Faster and faster, farther and farther, he threw stones. Perhaps it was a brother that gave him his first sling. Regardless, slinging stones became his obsession. Day after day, bear after bear, lion after lion, David lived to sling stones. As a shepherd, he learned to study a situation carefully. He noticed the details others missed. He studied the stance of his sheep's enemies. He could read the pasture like the best leaders of our day read the room. He grew more intuitive, perceptive, and confident. He found his strength in his bias for action.

Do you know your bias? Your bias will connect you to the opportunities God brings your way. Is your bias service to others? Leadership? Problem solving? Engineering or fixing things? Encouraging others? I'm not talking about personality findings. I'm talking about what really makes you tick! I'm asking you - *what jerks your chain? What brings you to life?* More to the point, *how do you see yourself in an opportunity? Do you quickly assume the position of who you really are in unfamiliar moments?* The short answer is that our biases are grounded in our strengths. *What are your greatest strengths? What opportunities could benefit from your strengths? What if you pursued opportunities that need your bias?* Again, *do you know your bias?* We'll come back to it. Meanwhile, let's return to David.

Lions and bears had been his *familiar* until the day he delivered the cheese to his brothers. That's the day everything changed. To David's brothers and King Saul, Goliath remained an unsurmountable obstacle. David's bias for action overrode the bias of all the king's men for inaction. His proven skills in the shepherd's field promoted him in the battlefield. Proven skills usually do. *Are you proving your strengths in the 'shepherd's field' so you'll be ready for the battlefield?*

What opportunity is taunting you to take it? The challenge of an opportunity is never the problem. The problem is always how we see ourselves. It's always in how we think about ourselves. It's a faith challenge, not a fear challenge. David's brothers and King Saul calculated Goliath's threat as a fear challenge. David saw his threat as a faith challenge. Maybe David thought, *could he be who he really was in the unfamiliar and scattered world of the battlefield? Should he just go back to the shepherd's field?*

Because the challenge offered by Goliath struck at the core of David's strengths and faith, he armed himself to meet the challenge. He had a real bias for fighting enemies that defied his God. It all began in the field with sheep threated by lions and bears. Hearing Goliath's threats drew him into the fray of the opportunity. Knowing our biases will do the same. *Do you see opportunities through your bias?*

David's transitional season to become the King of Israel began that day in Goliath's deadly shadow. His transitional season would linger for years. It would try everything within him for longer than anyone expected. His toughness would grow forward until he became the transformational version of himself needed for the throne. His transitional season scattered and shook him. The unfamiliar drove him beyond his comfort zone. His old *familiar*, literally the shepherd's field, would be forever left behind.

CONVERSATIONS IN OUR HEAD ARE GAME CHANGES

Toughness in our life challenges how we see ourselves in any moment. Here's the verse you may be expecting me to use: ***As a man thinks in his heart, so is he.*** (Proverbs 23:7) Here's my bluntness that you're not expecting. We have to get over ourselves to grow ourselves. We have to become who we need to be in the transitions of our scattered moments. We can't pander to our familiar. We have to look ourselves in the eye and talk trash to Satan's version of us. Our inner conversations about ourselves matter.

We're the gatekeeper of our thought life. How we talk to ourselves about ourselves either prepares us for the tough challenges ahead or schools us to fold to an avalanche of disappointments and excuses. Either way, they are pivotal points. *Which direction will you turn in the uncomfortable and unfamiliar intersections of your life? Will you choose preparation for challenges or schooling in disappointments and excuses?* Your choice. My choice, too.

Pivotal points in life either enlighten us or give escape from the moments we were created to own. Enlightenment or escape? Escape is comfortable. Enlightenment is challenging. We interpret opportunity according to our personal bias.

It's invigorating when we see opportunities as necessities because we have a bias (strength) to tackle them. It's dismissive of our bias not to. Discuss with yourself the following questions:

- *Where's the vacuum in your life that opportunity can fill?*
- *What strength is lying dormant in you that is your true self?*
- *What do you continually push to the back of your mind?*
- *Where have you settled for convenience sake, rather than for growth's sake?*
- *Where is your true north in this season of your life?*

JUMPING SHIP

Whenever a transition is in full play, there are risks. Risks? Yes, of course. We may totally miss our original target, because what we thought was the real target, isn't! We have to adapt. It's a juggling act. You may consider abandoning the challenges of a transition in one moment and be totally thrilled to be a part of it in the next. It seems like a crap shoot. Jumping ship in the middle of an uncomfortable challenge usually means missing the boat we were created to sail. When life is the most uncomfortable, it is human nature to jump ship. We grow weary of learning because it requires one paradigm shift after another. Faltering at this junction will cause us to grow distant from what we were supposed to become.

Opportunity is not just about us. Deep down we know that. But lost in the foggy mist of what we thought the opportunity was really about, we long to turn back to something more familiar. We'd rather be who we used to be and where we used to be. Life was simpler. We prefer simple. But there's a bigger picture in every opportunity. Seeing an opportunity is one thing. Fully understanding it is different. We have to stretch forward in more than one direction.

Here's what I've learned. First, opportunities require a decision. In fact, they bring us through revolving doors of decisions. Those revolving doors become our new normal. An indecisive nature will limit and keep us in neutral. We have to decisively push ourselves forward. We have to honestly answer the questions swirling in our head. We have to make decisions even when their timing seems abrupt and unfair. The pressure of the times does its best to force us to throw in the towel. Blinded by the emotions and fears of an unknown future, we are tempted to slide backward. We favor yesterday's comfort zones and the best practices that characterized them. We play with packing everything up and going back home. As Captain Hook said in the movie "Hook," that's *Bad form*!

2

THE OPPORTUNITY PRINCIPLE: DISCOVERY

Chase the complex and yet extraordinary
opportunities of this life
—Erik Wahl

What opportunity is staring you in the face? And what are you going to do about it? More importantly, what kind of environment do you need in order to thrive? Opportunity is not always about money. In fact, at the outset of our careers, it's about combining what we can bring to an opportunity and what an opportunity can bring to us.

If you're in a scattered time where there seems to be zero options, I guarantee you that there are opportunities waiting for you to discover. Don't procrastinate. You'll never see them if you're wearing outdated prescription glasses from your past. You have to want to see them. How? How, in scattered times, can you learn to see opportunities at your doorstep? Great question.

LIFE-GIVING OPPORTUNITIES

**Opportunity generates movement,
or it's just maintenance.**

Do you realize that life-giving opportunities generate movement? I've found that opportunity comes as a set of circumstances that initiate movement to do something…to become something…to make a difference. **Life-giving opportunities** generate movement, but they don't always start that way.

The life-giving nature of an opportunity often hides, especially in scattered times. That's why we have to look beyond the surface of our circumstances. We have to see life from different angles. We have to search for their potential until possibilities come out of hiding. How do life-giving opportunities generate movement? Here's what I've learned. Something begins to move within us. We become intrigued, even compelled to follow through. We explore the opportunity. We ask questions and do research. **Movement engages us mentally, spiritually, and relationally.**

First - Mentally. When we can't shake opportunities from our consciousness, we turn them over and over in our minds. Life-giving opportunities intrigue us mentally. We lean in. We imagine. We run the pros and cons and play optional scenarios. We research and explore beyond what's predictable. The inward dialogue in our mind initiates fresh conversations. We can't shut up. We speak up. We improvise where this opportunity might take us. Mentally, we fully engage. Life-giving opportunities eventually challenge us in other areas. We expect that. We want that. We want to go there. The movement of a life-giving opportunity also engages us spiritually.

Secondly - Spiritually. We engage our faith in the mix of what's moving within us. Faith backs us up to square one and challenges our motives. This is where we doubt ourselves. We lean into the wisdom of God's Word. We meditate and wait to see if the opportunity and our faith are compatible. Don't miss that point. Whenever God's peace rests upon a life-giving opportunity, movement accelerates. In our mind it's a done deal. But still we wait. We allow our emotions to calm down. We weigh the life-giving force of an opportunity both mentally and spiritually. We wait with prolonged patience! Why? Because a life-giving opportunity is not just about us. Movement includes people, all kinds of people. It always does. That's when movement engages us relationally!

Thirdly - Relationally. Compatibility of our vision and our people matter. Our vision for the opportunity must align with the right people. Only the right people take it forward. Movement relationally is in the character, creativity, and resourcefulness of the right people. Movement doesn't major on repeating history. Movement focuses on making history. Fragile relationships will abort movement. Our current inner circle of relationships may need to shift. In that shifting we are drawn to two kinds of people:

Maintenance people and Movement people.

Life-giving opportunities require both. Maintenance provides the launch pad for movement. To keep the *life* in a life-giving opportunity, we have to move strategically. Thus, we search for both kinds of people. Study the ministry of Jesus and you'll find both! His ministry was surrounded by both maintenance people (everyone usually named Mary!) and movement people (everyone called disciple).

The women that traveled with Jesus maintained the routine requirements for a traveling ministry. Their fulfillment in life was serving. They made sure the necessities were provided. The disciples were into on-the-job-training. Jesus was teaching them how to lead, follow, learn, and regroup as necessary. They were a work in the making, and they knew it. Following their master kept them in a constant flux of transformation. Their fulfillment was in becoming like Him.

Let's review. At first, a life-giving opportunity may seem unassuming and distant. It is the nature of an opportunity to conceal its full potential so as not to overplay its hand. If we live wanting to see them, we live expecting to see them. When we embrace them, things start happening. Life-giving opportunities move us mentally, spiritually, and relationally. They are strategic. They trick us into investing ourselves in them. Opportunities of the God-kind have every intention of changing us. They bring life-giving challenges to our table. Our imagination soars. Anything stagnant within us either comes back to life or is dismissed. We find ourselves fully engaging in transition. One moment, we may doubt that an opportunity is the right opportunity, but in another, we can't shake it out of our mind. The truth is that opportunities that don't challenge us, won't change us. Movement is in the challenge. Change is in the movement. Remember, transitions are prequels to transformation. Movement matters.

SEEING, SEIZING AND NAVIGATING OPPORTUNITY

Seeing, seizing, and navigating is impossible if we blind ourselves to the opportunities around us. How do we blind ourselves to opportunities? Here's what I've learned more than once.

In unfamiliar times, our thoughts tend to run the gamut of unbridled emotions. Unbridled emotions bounce from moments of excited expectation to bursts of anger and prejudice. Anger and prejudice are usually aimed at the new cultural environments and people that seem to be stifling our opportunity. The truth is that our thoughts are constantly consumed with what's wrong with the environment and people surrounding us. It's like sitting at an intersection with the traffic lights changing but we're not moving.

Why do we become consumed with this line of thought? Simple. We miss the environment and people of our past familiar! We grieve. Our brokenness is taken out on those around us. Their shortcoming is that they happen to be different from where we came. They live in environments that are different. Bottom line: **We aren't ready to change!** James understood this on a personal level. Tradition claims that James didn't believe Jesus was the Messiah until after the resurrection. More about that later.

Anger and prejudice are the blinders that obscure the opportunities in front of us. Judgmental conversations leave us blindsided. When this happens, we fall into the unhealthy comparison gap. We say we're looking for opportunities, but we're part-timers in that pursuit. Why? Because our focus is diverted. Why? Because our thinking is unbridled. We live playing the comparison game between our past and our present.

When our thought life carries unchecked baggage from our past, we need someone to help us take the blinders off and do the hard work. Seeing, seizing, and navigating opportunity requires staying focused on the main goal. As the Apostle Paul wrote to the Philippians, we have to neglect things that are behind us in order to stretch toward what's ahead. We know this truth, but we live life relearning it.

My default scripture in scattered times always comes back to this one:

> *Commit your work to the Lord and He will establish your thoughts.*
>
> PROVERBS 16:3 (KJV)

When we aren't 100% committed to seeing, seizing, and navigating opportunities, neither are our thoughts. When judgement and anger take passive ownership of our thinking, things get out of order. We may have faith in one direction, but our unbridled emotions take us in another. Our quest for opportunity is compromised. Our thinking is unstable. We're scattered.

The Psalmist found himself in a similar position. In Psalm 119:133 (NIV), he prays:

> *Order my steps in your word, let no iniquity have domin-*
> *ion over me. Redeem me from human oppression, that I*
> *may obey your precepts.*

Combining these two scriptures in Proverbs and Psalms brings us to the conclusion that in unfamiliar times, we need order, not disorder. In our thinking, order begins when we commit our work to the Lord. This includes how we see, seize and navigate opportunities in our thinking. The combined promise of these two scriptures assures us that God stands ready to reform our thoughts and reorder our steps. But first, we have to commit our work to Him. This commitment must have a stickiness that keeps on sticking. We need ordered steps.

GOD ORDERS OUR STEPS

His Ordering of our steps realigns our thinking with God's Word. For people of faith, God's ordering of our lives initiates life-giving habits. They keep us expectantly watching for new **o**pportunities, **r**elationships, **d**isciplines, **e**nvironments, and **r**esponsibilities. **(O.R.D.E.R.)**

This is an acronym that helps us remember that God is there for us to the point that He orders into my life a constant parade of options and disciplines. It's part of His *passionate investment.* It keeps us expectant in scattered times. I live expecting the following five things from Him, but not necessarily in this order. Before I go into detail, survey these five and note what's lacking in your life. Do you welcome:

Opportunities that **Challenge** your previously self-imposed boundaries and limitations?

Relationships that **Circumvent** your previously self-serving inner circle of influencers?

Disciplines that **Confront** previously self-indulged versions of your potential?

Environments that **Conflict** with previously self-assumed views of the world's needs?

Responsibilities that **Change** previously self-limiting skillsets to meet those needs?

GOD ORDERS OUR STEPS TO MEET THE NEEDS AROUND US.

GOD ORDERS OUR STEPS WITH:

1. Opportunities that challenge our self-imposed boundaries and limitations.

Every challenge we step into should change us. Previous challenges were meant to set us up for future ones. *Are your present moments continuing to change you? Are you allowing them to? If not, are you limiting yourself?*

Regardless of the volumes of experience that we bring to any agenda, we have to see life and its experiences with fresh eyes and challenge our self-imposed limitations.

> **No man steps into the same river twice. The river is never the same and neither is the man.**
>
> ANONYMOUS

2. Relationships that circumvent our self-serving inner circle of influencers.

Our inner circle of influencers has to change. Those who were major influencers in our past may become minor players in our future. That's ok. Influencers from yesterday's season may be out of season for where God's moving us next. Think of your high school inner circle. Anything changed? Of course, it has. Our inner circle is always changing.

Now matters. The shifting in the circle of influencers around us matters. Not just the people we listen to, but the books we read and other sources of input are always shifting. Relationships relevant for the 'now' must become our priority.

3. Disciplines that confront our self-indulged versions of our known potential.

Why do we settle for outdated versions of ourselves? Updated versions of ourselves depend on fresh disciplines and habits needed for the future version of ourselves. Updates do not conflict with who we are in Christ. Paul grew beyond his original understanding of himself and his purpose. Yesterday's habits may stagnate our thought processes. We have to renew our thinking beyond how we traditionally think of ourselves. Disciplines that don't maximize our strengths stalemate our potential. How we see ourselves in each new season should always be evolving. *What habits do you need to question? Change? Adopt? Update?*

4. Environments that Conflict with our self-assumed view of the world's needs.

New environments challenge the way we see the world's needs. Our way of meeting the needs of people around us requires a constant update of what our present world considers their greatest need. As our social culture evolves, our perception of their needs should change. God will sometimes shift our environments to keep us relevant. If we're not connected and knowledgeable of those changing environments, our lack of relevance will cost us. We can't meet a need we don't see. Thus, the opportunity to meet it becomes lost on us! Jesus practiced meeting practical needs. Doing so opened the door to meeting spiritual needs. Relevance in the times we live matters. Don't assume you're relevant. Live current to the environments the unspiritual world is facing. Listen to what they're talking about. Don't compromise the message but do update your verbiage and methods for presenting it.

5. Responsibilities that change our self-limiting skillsets for meeting those needs.

Skillsets that worked in the last opportunity may not be relevant in our new opportunity. Yesterday's familiar may not qualify us for the emerging new familiar. We may have to *go back to school!* Our skillsets and vocabulary may need updating. When handed responsibilities beyond our previous skillsets, we may fight or take flight. We have a choice to make. We either become relevant or allow the moment to kick us to the curb of irrelevancy. What we bring to the table of opportunity needs to be relevant to the scattered times we live. Applying sweat equity in the immediate grows us exponentially for the future. Procrastination in the immediate will not serve the future opportunity that God is unfolding.

It's easy to become so inwardly focused on our past strengths that we sacrifice opportunities on the altar of an 'I'm not ready yet' mindset. Somewhere, somehow, with someone, we must expand what we learned in the past to become relevant to what's in our present. As we put what we're learning into action, we may see 2 things:
1. Holes in our understanding and relevance.
2. Greater needs in the world around us.

Are you willing to let the opportunity in front of you change everything for you?

LOVING THE UGLY DUCKLING

Jesus saw opportunities because He lived to please His Father.

Remember when you first fell in love and lived to please that special person? Remember when you were consciously engaged in thinking of ways to please them? Whatever we love doing or whoever we love being with motivates us. We live on the search for opportunities to prove our love. Their interests become our interests. Their favorite things become our favorite things. Even things we didn't like before suddenly captivate our thinking.

When it comes to opportunities, the same is true. In fact, looking for a way to justify an awkward or difficult opportunity or to make it attractive is the nature of transitional times. Friends will say things like: *What, are you crazy? Are you telling me that what you said you couldn't do, you're doing? Who do you think you are? Eating our past words is humbling and often necessary.*

Sometimes opportunities are like a teenager dancing with the supposedly ugly duckling with whom no one else wants to dance! Beauty is in the eye of the beholder. Sometimes, however, opportunities are so difficult that they are difficult to love. They are ugly ducklings with whom no one wants to dance. James' letter gives us a clue on finding a way to love a once awkward opportunity. In the same breath, he teaches us how to engage positively through the process of going after it.

The following questions reel us in to answer the hard questions. Here they are:

1. *How can I love an opportunity that throws me into a difficult transition?*
2. *How can I make an awkward opportunity attractive to love?*

Here's the James 1:2-4 breakdown:

> **My fellow believers, when it seems as though you are facing nothing but difficulties, see it as an invaluable opportunity to experience the greatest joy that you can! For you know that when your faith is tested it stirs up power within you to endure all things.**

Ah, power in scattered times! Or did you focus on 'facing nothing but difficulties'?

Remember James' letter is written to a people scattered by religious persecution. They fled their homelands and at his writing were living among strangers. Everything around them was unfamiliar. Their steps were out of order. James challenged them to *experience the greatest joy that they can!* If his letter stopped there, his challenge would have leaned heavily on their will power. Fortunately, in the next sentence we read:

> *when your faith is tested it stirs up power within you*
> *to endure all things.*

The Biblical principle here is a spiritual truth. Revelation must be grasped by faith and put into action. God's power and revelation can transform an 'ugly duckling' into a life-giving opportunity. We fall in love! It takes time. Stars in our eyes? We take the plunge.

WHAT GIDEON LEARNED (JUDGES 6-7)

Faith is always tested. That includes faith in ourselves, faith in our abilities, and faith in our resources. Our faith in others, as well as our faith in God is tested.

When an angel backed Gideon up against the wall in a winepress, he was told to *'go in the strength he did have'*. He wasn't ready. Ever been there? I know I have.

In the presence of God all of Gideon's excuses eventually fell short, as excuses do. Remember Moses' excuses at the burning bush? 'I can't talk, I stutter', Moses said. For Gideon 'going in the strength he did have' was his starting point. It's that place where we gather what we do know and cautiously move forward. Everything begins with a starting point. Gideon's power at his starting point was small but it grew as he learned to trust in God. The ugly duckling of an opportunity became the love of his life. Transformation is the nature of God's power within us. If Gideon could grow in God's power to become a champion, so can we. We can begin with the power we do have.

Here's the big truth that should engage us: **When we're tested it stirs up power within us to endure all things!** That's a truth worth our rejoicing. That's why we can count it all joy. Before you throw out excuses for not buying into this, wait a minute. This is part of leveraging opportunity. Don't cut your power short by cutting your joy short.

Joy comes from knowing that God's power within us is sufficient for the testing of our faith. Joy responds to the potential of his presence and power stirring within us. The *invaluable opportunity* is the proving ground of our faith. Joy was also a theme in Apostle Paul's writings. In fact, in Philippians 3:1, Paul writes: "**...don't ever limit your joy or fail to rejoice in the wonderful experience of knowing our Lord Jesus.**"

When we limit our joy and rejoicing, we limit ourselves. Rejoicing carries us into the experience of the *invaluable opportunity.* Our expectations rise. God's power stirs within us. It's not about the source of the difficulty, but the source of His power. It's about seeing opportunity in the difficulty as a vehicle for more fully developing our endurance. Endurance is toughness. Opportunity is meant to upgrade our level of toughness. We have to toughen up. In Paul's letter to the Romans, he backs us in a corner:

> *...Even in times of trouble we have a joyful confidence knowing that our pressures will develop in us patient endurance. And patient endurance will refine our character, and proven character leads us back to hope. And this hope is not a disappointing fantasy, because we can now experience the endless love of God cascading into our hearts through the Holy Spirit who lives in us.*
>
> ROMANS 5:3-5

But! *Just let it go.* All the "buts" in the world will not build one ounce of endurance in your character. To think that Jesus' life on earth was a cake walk would be wishful thinking. In fact, Hebrews states that Jesus **'learned obedience in the things He suffered'!** (Hebrews 5:8) In Philippians, we find that Paul had to **'learn to be content in all things!'** Remember, Paul writes the Philippian letter from the confines of a prison. Paul refers here to times of abundance as well as in times of lack. Check it out in the context of Philippians 3:12, any translation.

In the Gospel of Matthew, Jesus challenges us to **'Take upon us His yoke and learn of Him.'** (Matthew 11:29) Yes, we all have more learning to do. The easy way isn't always the easy way. Real life doesn't allow us to copy someone else's test paper. We have to own the answer before we can live the answer. Difficulties are always a character issue. The invaluable opportunity in every experience is a learning curve that refines our character. The unfamiliar must become our new familiar. Transitions are character issues.

God wants to toughen us up. This chapter has focused on seizing opportunity in difficult and transitional times. Toughness is a reality truth! It's embedded in every opportunity. The big question is do we really want to toughen up? Do we want to refine our character or just go through the rest of our days as we are? We can live comfortable or we can thrive in a life-giving opportunity that challenges us. *Would you rather be a copy of who you think you are or become the original God intended you to be?* Let's go deeper.

Let's go back and conclude this chapter with David and Goliath. Opportunity met David in the battlefield, but not before opportunity met him in the shepherd's field. Life is a buildup of experiences and invaluable opportunities. Life is not about making lemonade out of lemons. That is old school and powerless. Life is about joyful expectations in the promise of endurance that stirs up God's power to mature our character.

Our problem: We usually live a life with depleted power. Such a life results from not toughening up to embrace life-giving opportunities. In scattered times, we need the Holy Spirit to father us from God's perspective. The next chapter will take you there. All scattered and unfamiliar times are warmups for the toughness needed in our next season.

TRANSITIONS ARE PREQUELS TO TRANSFORMATION

Faith in Jesus Christ as Lord and Savior transitioned me. The great exchange of my sin nature for God's righteousness through Jesus Christ transformed me. In every season a new toughness emerges from my faith in God's Word and the power of the Holy Spirit. My relationship with both toughens me whenever I allow them. And I must always allow them. So must you.

I am living proof that surrendering to a life of faith through a genuine relationship with Jesus Christ changes everything. In every transition of life, I find that God is passionately invested in growing me into His intended version of myself. Let me say that bolder.

> **GOD IS PASSIONATELY INVESTED IN US BECOMING SOMEONE WE COULD NEVER BE WITHOUT HIS DIRECTION AND INTERVENTION.**

How does He do this? Glad you asked. He engages us. Salvation is not a rescue mission. Salvation is allowing what we don't deserve, the sacrifice of Christ, to cleanse us from the sin nature that once separated us from Him. Salvation does more than restart our life.

Salvation changes our nature, forgives our past, and loves us into a working relationship with Almighty God! Salvation births in us a propensity to *go after Him!* Because of our faith in the new birth, we become the 'righteousness of God in Christ Jesus' (II Corinthians 5:21 KJV). We can't get that at a big box store. It's a gift. It's personal.

Jesus' life, death and resurrection are God's passionate investment in us. That investment is an eternal life investment. Eternal life ushers us into the movement of a life yielded to Him. Movements move, and thus we grow. He is not finished growing us at our conversion of faith. Believing that Jesus is who He says He is and in what He says He has done, rewrites our story. He moves the black and white screen shot of our past into our true identity. The journey is real.

DECISIONS DEFINE US. OPPORTUNITIES CHANGE US.

OPPORTUNITIES

- Do you see difficulties as invaluable opportunities?
- How astute are you to recognize opportunities?
- Do you see opportunities coming?
- Do you seek opportunities?
- Are you up to the challenge of opportunities?

DECISIONS

- How decisive are you?
- Do you live oblivious to your need to make decisions?
- What was the most important decision you made yesterday?
- Last year? As a young adult?
- Which decision did you make years ago that still benefits you today?

- Are you conscious of the long-range consequences of your decisions?
- What decisions do you need to make today?

Decisive people tackle more opportunities than most because they see more opportunities. We live a limited version of our life unless we see the opportunities staring us in the face. We have to learn to see them. Nothing resets the possibility scales in our favor like seeing and seizing opportunities.

3

THE OPPORTUNITY PRINCIPLE: HOLY SPIRIT, HABITS, AND CREATIVITY

Tourists see what they have come to see,
travelers see what there is to see.
—*Anonymous*

THE FATHERING NATURE OF THE HOLY SPIRIT

Jesus refers to the Holy Spirit as the Spirit of Truth. The *fathering* nature of the Holy Spirit stirs up power within us when we live engaged in a relationship with Jesus. In John 14:18 (NIV), he promises that He will not leave His disciples as 'orphans' or 'fatherless.' We can bank on His faithfulness to father us through life. The currency in our relationship with Jesus lives in the freshness of our relationship with the Holy Spirit, but we must allow His direction and intervention. He wants to father us!

The Gospel of John (14-16) includes Jesus' final teaching before the crucifixion. In these three chapters of John's Gospel, we discover the fathering nature of God as Jesus intended it to be through the Holy Spirit. The *why* behind Jesus sending the Holy Spirit comes down to teaching, guiding, comforting, and fathering believers. John gives us the intimate inside track found in no other Gospel. His text is a rich prelude to all that follows in early church history. Luke, writing in the Book of Acts, chronicles the Acts of the Holy Spirit through mostly first-hand experience. First century leaders had a penchant for tackling opportunity at every turn. They did so with both an inspirational and instructional goldmine through the Holy Spirit. We must welcome the direction and intervention of the Holy Spirit in our daily walk. The Holy Spirit is a gift of faith.

> *If you then, though you are evil, know how to give good gifts to your children, how much more will your Father in heaven give the Holy Spirit to those who ask Him.*
>
> LUKE 11:13 (NIV)

In this text from Luke's Gospel, we learn what Jesus taught his followers about receiving the Holy Spirit. Simply ask, He said. The challenge is for us keep His fullness in our life. He should be as present on our *battlefield* as He is in our *shepherd field*. Why? Because what we learn in our *shepherd field* is vital to our success on the *battlefield*. In scattered times, we tend to say that we just can't wait to get out of the *shepherd fields* in life. By *shepherd fields*, I refer to times that appear routine to the point of boredom or challenging to the point of panic. When life takes us to the *battlefield* of our next opportunity, we tend to long to go back to the familiar *shepherd field*! By the grace of God, David found life-giving opportunities more potent in the *battlefield*. God's plan for us in the *shepherd fields* is always to father and toughen us up for our next season. Likewise, the stirring of His power in us during scattered times in both fields is dual purposed: to prepare us to deal with the challenging times we're experiencing and prepare us to see the opportunities in those challenges.

An on-going relationship with the Holy Spirit is intended to be the constant in the variables we find in scattered and trying times. **Jesus saw opportunities because He lived to please His Father.** That included fluid conversations with His Father. Follow Jesus in any adventure in the Gospels, and you'll see how He cherry- picked opportunities that made the religious crowd cringe. It was like He plucked them out of thin air. His choices provided on-the-job training for His disciples and battle ground moments for Himself.

Holy Spirit opportunities also provide these dual benefits in our lives. There are several takeaways from this thought. **Never do life alone.** Allow the Holy Spirit to disciple you through your life while at the same time taking you through a battle to toughen you. The purpose of all transitions is always transformation.

HOW DID JESUS LEARN TO SEE OPPORTUNITIES?

It's not a stretch to realize that **Jesus saw opportunities to please his Father because He valued time with His Father.** In fact, He prioritized His life to spend time with the Father, especially in times that tested and could have scattered His focus.

Now let's pull that curtain back and rethink Jesus in the scattered and difficult times of His ministry. By scattered, I refer to times that could have unraveled the Father's plans. When we join his story, we realize His perspective was connected to a three-year timetable of ministry. One of His major pre-crucifixion agendas was discipling followers. Followers follow. They stick with you. They're always there. I repeat, *they are always there*, like 24/7 there! Traveling with our followers will toughen us up. If you've done it, you know it. Prolonged patience toughens us.

Here is an example of one of those times:

At the feeding of the 5,000, we find the 12 disciples in a panic. They've stared so intently at their lack of resources that they've become blinded. 'Send the people away' was the only solution the disciples could come up with! Isn't that our usual response to difficulties, 'make them go away.' 'No ugly ducklings' today, please.

But Jesus saw over 5,000 hungry people waiting! Cool? Yes, but that 5,000 only had five loaves of bread and two smelly fish. *Ugly duckling* times 5,000! At least that was the view of His closest 12 followers!

On the other side of the conversation, Jesus sought to know the creative base from which His disciples lived. He learned that day, if not before, that His followers' base of operation was limited to whatever was visually on hand. They were limited as well to their first solution to any problem. They lived limited by their familiar. Jesus transitioned them into an unfamiliar so he could transform them into the new familiar! Sound *familiar*?

With the 5,000, Jesus saw a miracle in and beyond the 5 loaves and 2 fish. That possibility totally escaped His disciples' level of thinking. They were clearly not on Jesus' wavelength. In difficult times throughout Jesus' ministry, He stayed focused on the potential within the crisis. That's more than a leadership principle; that's a character principle. It's one the Holy Spirit desires to father in us. The Holy Spirit does not come and go – He dwells. His presence broadens the field of opportunities beyond our sensory abilities. He never wastes a crisis, and neither should we.

When Jesus told the disciples 'you feed them,' He was already mentally engaged in mathematical division! He was thinking of how to divide the crowd of 5,000 plus women and children into groups of 50 or 100. He was doing the mathematics while the disciples were looking for an escape hatch. Jesus practiced seeing opportunities from His Father's perspective. That's a major practice we should engage in as well. We need the Holy Spirit to teach us how to see opportunities beyond the stats of the moment.

Jesus grew in stature, wisdom, and favor with God and man. That means He toughened up. We also know from the Hebrew writer that Jesus was tempted in every way that we are. He faced challenges, but He focused on opportunities to show off his Father!

Jesus never saw situations limited by the stats in the situation. Scripture tells us that He knew what He would do before He did it. He always saw opportunity in the plural. He also read the crowd differently than His followers. (Read John's account in John 6:1-15 for more details.)

'OPPORTUNITY HABITS' HAVE TO BE PRACTICED

Opportunity has to be practiced. Seeing opportunity is difficult, but even in scattered times, opportunity exists. It's a matter of developing **opportunity habits**. Jesus practiced seeing beyond the crisis in front of him. Back at the wedding in Cana, Jesus was not clueless on how to turn water into wine. He was processing the results of doing so. That's fair. That's part of practicing opportunity.

> *If I do this, it won't change anything for you, but it will change everything for me!*
>
> JOHN 2:4

From the Passion Bible Translation of John 2:4 we get a glimpse, not only into Jesus' thought processing but of the follow up to all creative solutions. Jesus seems to be asking the same things we need to ask when opportunity comes knocking:

- Will this opportunity change everything?
- Will it make my life more impactful or more difficult?
- How will it affect others?
- How will it affect the bottom line?
- Will it glorify God?
- What habits do I need to practice in order to see and seize opportunity?

6 OPPORTUNITY HABITS

Developing these habits will expand how you discover opportunities. Engage with the Holy Spirit as your partner and expect to see things differently. With Him you will see multiple opportunities and solutions where previously you saw only a few.

Habit #1: Look at Jesus' miracles with fresh eyes. Think about the story from different angles. Ask yourself who else was there and what else was going on. Ask why whatever was said was said. I'm talking about what it takes to see and seize opportunities. Here's another key: Get relational with Jesus through the fathering of the Holy Spirit. Learn Jesus. How? Develop the habit of drawing yourself into conversation with any scenario in the Gospels. Take the feeding of the 5,000, for instance. Ask questions. Search for the solutions. Back up the truckload of your religious training long enough to rethink scripture as first time visitors to the story. Look at them with fresh eyes. Welcome the Holy Spirit into your analysis. Keep the conversation going.

Habit #2: Solve problems by digging into their opportunities. Look for more than one solution. On that hillside 5,000 people came to hear Jesus speak. But Jesus knew what He would do. Yes, He would teach them, but He would also demonstrate His teaching in a practical way to touch them. Jesus was a problem solver. When people were hungry, He fed them. When people were condemned, He forgave them. When people needed healing, He healed them. When people were possessed, He delivered them. When people had questions, He answered them, although not always in the way expected.

Practicing opportunity has a lot to do with problem solving. You can learn to practice problem solving by studying how Jesus did it. Invite the Holy Spirit to help you see what you previously missed. How did Jesus come to his way of doing things? How did He learn this mindset? The Sunday School answer is that He spent time with the Father, and that is absolutely the truth. But stopping at that truth only leaves us at the threshold of greater answers. Have you ever noticed that Jesus was more than an answerer; He was a *questioner*. Let's go back into the Gospels and examine the details in a variety of situations where people came to Jesus. What do we find happening? People are asking questions. How does Jesus answer them? Usually with another question! Take the rich young ruler. Jesus asked him enough questions to help that young ruler know his own heart. The young ruler had to walk away. Why? He wasn't ready to follow Jesus. Jesus used questions to help people find the right answers already within them. We have to learn to ask better questions, but not just for better answers. Keep reading.

Habit #3: Ask questions of God, but also anticipate His questions for you! Where did Jesus learn the power of asking questions? With His Father, night after night. In the stillness of the quiet, no doubt Jesus, the Son, asked questions of God, the Father! Why? To get his Father's answers? Yes and no! More than answers, Jesus wanted to *know* the Father. Getting relational with Jesus is about getting to know Him. Getting answers is consequential. If we make spending time with Him a habit, we will begin to see opportunities the way He did. Our teacher is the Holy Spirit. Jesus is the subject.

Habit #4: Expect answers because you have the mind of Christ.
The apostle Paul tells the Corinthians that they have the mind of
Christ (I Corinthians 2:16). Exploring opportunities with the mind
of Christ is a practice. Learning the subtext under the text of any
story about Jesus will take your thought process forward. Seizing
opportunities requires asking questions relevant to the context of
the bigger picture. Learning to see the subtext under the text of
what Jesus said in the Gospels takes us into his way of thinking.
If anyone was ever really in this world but not of it, it was Jesus!
He navigated through trying times because of where He focused.
Realizing that we're scattered is not the answer. Traction in scattered
times leverages answers beyond the obvious. Learning the mind
of Christ will take us there.

**Habit #5: Leverage your perception of yourself from God's
Kingdom perspective.** Jesus balanced His redemptive purpose
with the perspective of the times. What were those times? God's
people lived badgered by both the powers of Roman occupation
and religious jurisdiction. It was stifling to live in such times. Fear
was palatable. Jesus found himself walking out His purpose in those
scattered and troubling times. He consciously lived on redemption's
timeline where people around him were **facing nothing but difficulties.** He exposed people to the *invaluable opportunities around
them to experience the greatest joy!* He did so from His perception
of Himself leveraged in His Father's Kingdom perspective.

In the courtroom of perspective, perception matters. Don't race over
those two words: perspective and perception. We, too, can find our
Father's perception of us in His greater perspective of the times
we're living in. We, too, can come to a greater understanding of our
purpose (perception of ourselves) even in scattered times. We need
to know more than the layout of the land (Father's perspective). We
have to see where we fit in the layout of the land (Our perception).
Again, our bias comes into play. Remember our bias in this book

is about what we are for, not about what are against. Play your bias (strength) into the opportunity you're seeing. See how you can best be a contributor in the moment you're living. Practice playing off your bias (strengths) in the unsolved problems around you. Make engaging with the fathering of the Holy Spirit more than a habit. Make it your preference in daily life.

With the fathering presence of the Holy Spirit, we always have the opportunity to see our perception of ourselves from our Father's perspective. What if you made it a habit?

Habit #6: Leverage curiosity in scattered times. Transitions are not limited to difficult times. Transitions can be of our own choosing. Take on the adventure of getting a college degree, and you'll find yourself in transition. Make a trip to a foreign nation with a language not your own, take up a sport that you've never played or join a new community organization and you're in a transition. In all of these examples, you can feel scattered. Scattered times must bring out your curiosity. What if you practiced curiosity as a habit? Learn to read the room! Navigate the opportunity. Give Jesus wiggle room in your life.

How can we seize opportunities even in unfamiliar times? How can we take the blindfold off panic? How can we see clearly the options pulling at us to stretch and grow ourselves forward? What prism of perspective do we need to look through? What habits should we develop before or in the midst of those times? Can we live tuned in to a God who is always focused on a Kingdom narrative? Can we see our purpose in His narrative? Do we want to? To be earthly good, we have to be spiritually minded! We need His perspective.

God is always focused on us within His Kingdom narrative.

JESUS' CREATIVE FORCE WITHIN US

Before this gets too serious, I want to remind you that Jesus is the creative force behind everything that was ever made! He knows how to connect with us. His Word is the creative force that is still holding everything together. Surely, He knows how to interrupt our default habits and get us back online. John reminds us of this. It is written of Jesus that *through his creative inspiration this Living Expression made all things, nothing has existence apart from Him.* (John 1:3) The word translated here for Jesus is 'Living Expression.'

Jesus is the creator of all things: It's in His nature to be creative. We're made in His image: There is a creative force within every human being. By creative, I mean far more than what we normally think. The pigeonholed version of creativity leaves us with only a visual concept of artists. That limits our imagination to a job description and a talent. It robs us of a perception of ourselves as one made in the creative image of God. For *such a time as this*, let's dig deeper into this thought.

Creativity is always a game changer. Jesus was prone to creative miracles. As school age children, we scribbled in Crayola colors until the day we realized that our scribbles wouldn't be on our teacher's test. Slowly, answers for the teacher's tests became the only game in town. At that moment, most of us succumbed to the practicality of a lifestyle that worked without creativity. That doesn't mean creativity is not still resident in us. It just means we need to reembrace our old friend from our Crayola days.

How can we embrace this level of identity in Christ? Perhaps we need to allow our practical way of thinking to share equal space with creative thinking? Jesus was not one dimensional. He imagined. He developed parables day in and day out. Sometimes His parables had been completely thought out before hand and other times they were spontaneous. Why? How? Because Jesus was as habitually creative as He was pragmatic. He was also habitually improbable! He defied religious standards because He saw their hollowness and pretense. Remember Jesus driving out the money changers? How about that coin in a fish's mouth? How about forgiving that prostitute before she repented? He colored outside the lines. From a Kingdom narrative these actions weren't weird; they were strategic game changers.

What if we reset our mindset by processing thoughts as Jesus did? His nightly conversations with His father brought to surface everything His father had put into Him. Spending time with His Father toughened Him, but they also kept Him creative. Jesus learned to see multiple opportunities in a single walk through the crowd. That's creativity of the God kind! Jesus lived to show off His Father. So should we.

The reality of an opportunity is never void of creativity if we learn to think of creativity as an extension of problem solving. Jesus solved problems. Blindness was a problem, as was leprosy and paralysis. With creative thinking, we learn to see. We search for answers to questions no one else is asking. Why? Because we're curious. Curiosity is the gateway to revelation, healing, direction, and invention. When people tell me that they don't have a creative bone in their body, I know that they aren't dialing into their God-given curiosity. As a people created in the image of God, how could we ever deny that there are *creative bones* in us!? Awaken curiosity, and you will awaken creativity. Study the life of Christ and the early church and awaken the power of God within you.

What should we search for? What if we search for options usu-ally left on the curb by our tendency for more practical options? When Godly creativity is not trending in our thinking, we need to unthink, rethink, and renew our thinking. That should sound familiar. (Romans 12:1-2) Conforming to the norms of this world, we live substandard to the way Jesus processed His life. There are more options in every opportunity than our average attempts to find them. Fellowship with Jesus is serious business for those hungry to live on the creative edge to life. Out of shape with creativity? Practice curiosity. Allow the Holy Spirit to unlock opportunities. Hang out with others on the same quest.

A creative exercise: (Either enjoy the exercise, or skip to the next page)

Draw a large box in the center of a blank sheet of paper. Inside the box, write every normal possibility you know that would solve your existing problem, challenge, or opportunity. You should need a larger piece of paper for the next part.

Once you've exhausted what you know to be the normal options to your situation, begin writing wild and crazy solutions *outside the box*. Give yourself permission to get a little crazy. Your out-of-the-box ideas should be without the limitations of time, resources, and reality. Let me repeat that. ***Out of the box ideas should not be limited to your known inventory of time, resources, or reality.***

Wait, you're still not there. Don't put the pencil down. The point is to practice curiosity and creativity spontaneously. Tax your curiosity, not your brain! This is not a common-sense exercise. This exercise should prove that without a deadline, limited resources, or allegiance to reality, we think differently. Small thinking throws limitations with such a force that curiosity leaves the room. Don't be judge and jury to any creative thoughts in the moment of their arrival. Take time later to explore and evaluate them, but not at their conception.

Once you do this exercise, you may discover that your way of thinking needs a creative recharge! Thinking outside the proverbial box of common sense and predictability runs crossways to logic. I'm not saying God is not logical or practical. I am saying that's not all that He is. But practicing creativity will put you in a closer proximity to the way God thinks. If you want to reconnect with curiosity and creativity, you have to practice it. It's best practiced through time with Jesus through the Holy Spirit. Here's a scripture that backs up the fact that there's always more to be discovered than we've discovered so far.

> *This is why the Scriptures say: Things never discovered or heard of before, things beyond our ability to imagine – these are the many things God has in for all his lovers. But God now unveils these profound realities to us by the Holy Spirit. Yes, he has revealed to us his inmost heart and deepest mysteries through the Holy Spirit, who constantly explores all things.*
> I Corinthians 2:9-10

While these verses certainly include the mystery of our salvation, they are not limited to it. Verse 15 in the Passion Bible Translation brings even more clarity to what Paul writes about at length in this text.

> *Those who live in the Sprit are able to carefully evaluate all things, and they are subject to the scrutiny of no one but God.*
> I Corinthians 2:15

Problem solving begins in the practice of creative thinking even when there's not a crisis. In our quiet times with the Lord, we find ourselves more receptive to His out-of-the-box solutions and perspectives. Why else did Jesus tell us to ask, seek, and knock? He created us to live curiously!

God scrutinizes the validity of what we think in line with His Word. He searches for the value in what we're thinking. In His out-of-the-box solutions and perspectives, we gain a fresh perception of ourselves. It really matters how we see ourselves in Christ. In studying scripture, we should expect wisdom and revelation beyond the mere words on the page. Paul prayed this for believers in Ephesus.

> *I pray that the Father of Glory, the God of our Lord Jesus Christ, would impart to you the riches of the Spirit of wisdom and the Spirit of revelation to know him through your deepening intimacy with him. I pray that the light of God will illuminate the eyes of your imagination, flooding you with light, until you experience the full revelation of the hope of his calling – that is, the wealth of God's glorious inheritances that he finds in us, his holy ones!*
>
> EPHESIANS 1:17-18

Paul learned to scrutinize scriptures through the Holy Spirit. The Holy Spirit as teacher, teaches. He expects us to be life-time learners. The Holy Spirit as leader, leads. Let the Holy Spirit become all that Jesus said the Holy Spirit is. Take some time to reread and study the teachings of Jesus on the Holy Spirit in John 14, 15 & 16.

PAUL & THE PRISON WALLS OF OPPORTUNITY

Paul's revelation had a creative edge. The apostle Paul saw the opportunity in prison to write letters to the churches he had started. What he may have taught in person, became letters. They were full of Holy Spirit revelation. Revelation has a creative edge. They began as an idea in the confines of a prison cell. Trapped in prison could have left Paul feeling scattered. But the theme of Paul's writings always came back to rejoicing, especially in tough times. Rejoicing toughens us because it goes against the grain of default thinking and normal exposé of feelings. Paul learned to think thoughts in scattered and disruptive environments. So can we. His bias was teacher. Prison time didn't cancel out his bias to teach; neither should scattered times cancel out our bias. Like flood waters in the natural world, our bias should always find a way to flow.

MAKE YOUR RELATIONSHIP WITH JESUS TRULY RELATIONAL. HOW? ASK QUESTIONS. GET ANSWERS. ALLOW HIM TO INTERRUPT YOUR NORMAL. ALLOW HIM TO DISTURB YOU IN THE GOOD TIMES AS WELL AS THE SCATTERED. MAKE IT A HABIT TO LIVE CURIOUS. SEEK OUT LIFE-GIVING ENVIRONMENTS. LIVE FULLY ALIVE TO HIS PRESENCE.

Let's walk this truth out into the sunlight. Generating creative thinking should be an intentional part of our life. Why? It's in line with how God created us. Chasing ideas is the avenue of creativity. Not every idea is creative, but at their least they generate options. Quit brainstorming and start idea-generating. Brainstorming is usually limited to things we already know, like rearranging deck chairs on the Titanic as it's sinking. Idea-generating explores the unknown possibilities. Creative thinking is a starting place. Process 'what if' solutions and ideas in your life as you live it. Why? Let's go back to the major theme of this book:

GOD IS PASSIONATELY INVESTED IN DEVELOPING US INTO SOMEONE WE COULD NEVER BECOME WITHOUT HIS DIRECTION AND INTERVENTION.

The more like Jesus we become, the more *passionately invested* we also become in developing into someone we could never be without God's direction and intervention. Thinking for a change rather than for a repeat of yesterday has to become habit. Yesterday's solutions are limited. They easily trap us into the quagmire of the same old brand of problem solving.

Imagine what you could think if you really believed that you could hear from God? Imagine seeing life through a different set of eyes? His! Imagine. Imagine. Imagine.

4

THE OPPORTUNITY PRINCIPLE: THE TOURIST VS TRAVELER MINDSET

*The traveler sees what he sees;
the tourist sees what he has come to see.*
— *G. K. Chesterton*

TOURISTS SEE WHAT THEY'VE COME TO SEE.

When we live life as a tourist, we only see what we've been told to see. Our tour guide routes us through the same popular venues that every other tourist expects. We check off duplicate bucket lists in line with what all the other tourists saw.

TRAVELERS SEE DIFFERENTLY. HOW?

1. Traveler's believe there's **more** to see than what's common. Therefore, they research *more*, go behind the scenes of history *more*, and ask unsettling questions *more* to get beyond the *less*. They think as travelers at all times, familiar and unfamiliar. It's a habit.
2. Travelers believe they can find *more* if they think curiously, like an explorer.

3. Travelers play off the influencers around them who have a similar curiosity and explorer bias.

Do they run into dead ends? Yes. Explorers maintain their curiosity with and without discovering something new. Curiosity is in their blood. At the heart of their curious mindset is the habit of reflective thinking. Creativity thrives in reflective thinking. Is reflective thinking one of your habits? Reflective thinking facilitates reviewing on a regular basis what's working well and what's not. Reflective thinking brings us back to reevaluating options that require more reflective time. Reflective thinking is the most powerful when done with the Holy Spirit.

Let me ask you something. Do you think that Jesus, as creator for the universe, had only one idea for creating a tree? Not if you look at the world around you. What about mountains? No, again. Having visited the Canadian Rockies as well as the Great Smokey mountains, I know the reality is that the Creator certainly had more than one great 'mountain' idea. What about people? No, again. Sometimes there is more than one answer, even more than one opportunity. Think about it. Reflect on it.

QUESTIONS TO PONDER
- Why do we limit opportunities and solutions to the first thing that pops into our minds?
- Why do we limit how we solve problems to only previous solutions?
- Why do we limit our curiosity to only brainstorming, instead of idea generating?
- Why do we limit how we see others based upon who they remind us of?
- Why do we to live a version of ourselves that limits our understanding of ourselves?

- Why do we limit our curiosity to what others worked in the past?
- Why are we so unprepared for scattered or unfamiliar times? You guessed it!

CHALLENGING OUR STATUS QUO IDEAS

Processing a fresh pool of ideas is healthy. Recycling stale thinking is unhealthy. A preset mindset of *'If life goes this way, I'll do this, and if life goes that way, I'll do that'* can be limiting not because the ideas are not feasible, but because they may no longer be relevant.

For example, most of Jesus' disciples grew up with a bias for carpentry or fishing. Only Matthew, the tax collector, challenged that status quo. Jesus' transition from carpenter was a gutsy move for the average man of His day, especially at the age of 30! Think about it. Jesus was not average. He could have been anything. What happened?

LEANING AND LEARNING

Jesus' insistence that John baptize Him was the predictable outcome of years and years of learning and leaning into His Heavenly Father's *line of work!* Please note that He both leaned and learned. (Proverbs 3:5-6) Leaning is a trust factor. His evolving habits of leaning and learning into conversations with His Father set in motion the platform for His decision making. Likewise, the conversations we lean into and learn from scripture become the platforms on which we make decisions.

Trust in the Lord with all your heart, and do not lean on your own understanding. In all your ways acknowledge him and he will make straight your paths.
PROVERBS 3:5-6 (ESV)

Most suppose Jesus spent nights in prayer only once His ministry began. But that assumption carries the same level of legitimacy as thinking that David had never slung rocks before confronting Goliath! How we process our ways of thinking in times not scattered will carry over into scattered times. How we see ourselves in familiar times will also carry over into unfamiliar times, as well. Seizing an opportunity if restricted to how we've always thought or seen ourselves will generate fewer options. Living curiously keeps the options coming when the Holy Spirit is our teacher, guide, and father.

OUR IDENTITY MATTERS

Habitually seizing and navigating opportunities should raise our thinking level to whatever is needed. How we identify ourselves should be flexible enough for us to transition into whatever paradigm shift God's perspective requires.

'Joseph and Mary's son' had once been Jesus' identity, but the baptismal waters changed His identity in line with how He changed His habits. John the Baptist immediately declared Jesus the '*Son of God who takes away the sins of the world.*' Following baptism, Jesus went into the wilderness to be tested. Temptations tested Him for 40 days and nights. At the end of that time of testing, Jesus returned in the power of the Holy Spirit. He moved forward with well measured steps toward his ultimate destiny. Everything began to accelerate. His identity expanded. How He saw himself changed. The shift in His identify affected both His outward practices and inward thinking. That's why at the wedding the Passion Bible translates Jesus' words:

> *If I do this, it won't change anything for you, but it will change everything for me!*

JOHN 2:4

Jesus was seeing Himself differently before the water into wine miracle. It wasn't so much that He reinvented Himself, but that He was walking in a new perspective of the Holy Spirit's power. Recognizing the power of God within us changes how we see ourselves. Because of his power shift after the wilderness experience, Jesus saw Himself and the times He was living differently. His world view changed. He knew turning water into wine would accelerate the paradigm shift in how others saw Him. He knew this because He spent relational times with His Father. He didn't take a poll of popular opinions. Neither should we. Our expectations should be offshoots of our relational times with the Holy Spirit.

Our identity changes when we spend time with Him. It has to. It is purposed to. It's a vital part of how we navigate opportunities in scattered times. This shift is not a pride thing, but a servant thing. We serve God differently as our identity in Christ becomes clearer.

With a new identity and a renewed mind, we naturally rejoice in trying times that momentarily scatter us. Knowing that *the trying of our faith* works to our advantage, we watch for new angles by which to leverage life. We rejoice in God before the breakthroughs happen because we know something is coming. We expect power updates! Endurance updates! Toughness updates! Character updates! Encouragement updates!

ONE-DIMENSIONAL LIFE

In all of His ways of thinking, Jesus was Spiritual perfection. How did He become that? He owned His daily moments through the identity He learned during times with His Father. He never lived a one-dimensional version of Himself. He lived habitually engaged in who and what made Him Jesus.

THREE THINGS WE HAVE TO GRASP TO LIVE FULLY IN OUR GOD GIVEN IDENTITY:

1. **Who we are in Christ** – Righteousness, dearly loved children, followers of Jesus
2. **Who He is in us** – Redeemer, Savior, Healer, Peace, Joy, Holy Spirit's presence
3. **Why we're on the planet** – To attract people to Jesus, even those nothing like Him.

A COUPLE OF MORE QUESTIONS FOR YOU:

- *Is it the lack of integrating a variety of ways of thinking that leaves you scattered?*
- *Are you so one dimensional in your thinking that you cut yourself short?*

In the Gospels, we see Jesus speaking differently depending on the moment. He obviously utilized different thought bases at different times. One moment He is speaking with great authority and the next He is speaking with great compassion. My point is that our identity in Christ Jesus means we can think from different angles of thought about the opportunities around us. We can speak from an authority base one minute and a more passionate base the next. We can think as travelers. Jesus was a traveler. We are travelers. The Gospel was generated by travelers. They lived, thought, and spoke beyond a tourist mentality. They came to life every day to see what there was to see. That's how they changed the world.

Paul was a traveler, but he wasn't one dimensional. He was at once an academic, a strategist, a teacher, a preacher, a writer, an intercessor, and at the same time *just Paul!* All of these helped make him Paul. In all of them, he knew who he was in Christ, who Christ was in him, and why he was on the planet. The same multifaceted analogy can be made of Jesus. Jesus was the 360 degree version of Himself as God intended Him to be! Yes, He was divine, but yes, He was human. He was teacher, prophet, storyteller, miracle worker, redeemer, and son of Joseph and Mary all at the same time.

> *He understands humanity, for as a Man, our magnificent King-Priest was tempted in every way just as we are, and conquered sin. So now we come freely and boldly to where love is enthroned, to receive mercy's kiss and discover the grace we urgently need to strengthen us in our time of weakness.*
> HEBREWS 4:15-16

Jesus was touched by the same weaknesses that touches us today. It follows that in His understanding of humanity, he was also touched by opportunities that touch us. As a traveler, Jesus saw, each day, what there was to see. His life proves beyond a shadow of doubt that as temporarily residents on earth, our best life is lived as a traveler, not as a tourist. We must come to every day as travelers. By His presence in us, we come to see what there is to see from God's point of view. We don't live life just seeing what everyone else expects us to see.

What is it you're not seeing about who God made you? How can you see more clearly the variety of opportunities within the moments you're living? Are you limited by your curiosity? Your creativity? Your thinking? Your identity? Think about it. Grow your curiosity beyond your predictable tastes and trendy thinking. Find some new expressions, stories and ideas. Read books, attend events, meet people and volunteer outside your normal tendencies. Expand your vocabulary.

Jesus traveled. He talked with people with whom He wasn't expected to talk. He partied with people with whom He wasn't supposed to party. Wherever He went, He found a way to be His relevant self! He connected with life as it was happening around Him by transitioning fully into the opportunities before Him. He fully owned His moments. He welcomed the interruptions and movement of the Holy Spirit. Again, He was at once prophet, teacher and miracle worker because each of them played a role in Jesus being Jesus.

Jesus had a great memory for details, but He also had a great imagination. His scope of understanding was multi-dimensional within all generational and people groups. Spiritually, Jesus knew what was in the heart of mankind individually and collectively. He wisely took His conversations forward to meet the needs of their hearts and challenge the conflicts in their thinking.

Jesus learned to monitor what was happening in the minds around Him and at the same time, what the Holy Spirit was streaming through His thinking.

> *Whatever builds up your faith and deepens your love must become your holy pursuit.*
> II TIMOTHY 2:22B

See opportunity as inherently yours as a traveler. The powers of God flow best through the traveler mentality as demonstrated in the lives of Abraham, Isaac, Jacob, Joseph, Moses, and the countless others. They learned to see, seize and navigate their way through life as travelers by following the purposes and plans God revealed to them by the Holy Spirit.

Today's a great day to believe that you are who God says you are and that you can do what He says you can do in the moment you are living. Leverage opportunities as if you owned them until you do. Live as travelers.

ASKING QUESTIONS

Who do you know that thinks circles around you? Spend time with them! Pick their brain. Question their way of thinking. Broaden your circle of influencers. Investigate what makes the most fascinating people in your life tick. If you have to, pay them to spend time with you. Invest yourself in conversations without a fear that your limited tourist minded thinking will be discovered by a life-giving Traveler! Live your transitions as a Traveler until your transformation is complete. Travelers are the most exciting *sights* you will ever see!

We only have today's timeline to influence the world around us. Hesitation does not wear well on the curious. Inferiority does not excuse us from being an explorer. Be child-like enough to ask *stupid* questions. Expect to gather brilliant answers. Then apply them in multiple areas of your life, not just one.

Here's a simple example of how I learned to ask the right questions.

THE DIRT ROAD STORY

When I was a child, we lived on a dirt road in central Florida. It was a dusty one lane or a graded two-lane depending on the moment. From elementary through high school, everyone on my dirt road asked out loud with a *touristy* mindset:

'When are they going to pave this road?'

Shortly after high school graduation, a friend of mine told me of a part-time job that would allow flexible hours with my college schedule. I applied and got the job. The job was typing right-away descriptions for the Marion County Road Department! Working with the right-away agent, I became curious enough to ask: **'How can we get our dirt road paved?'** The answer was simple. All we had do to was get a petition signed by the residents on our road! *What? That was it?* Yes, that was it!

I got our road paved because I asked the *right question* of the *right person.* The opportunity to get our road paved had always been there. But we had lived in a bubble asking the same old wrong questions of the same old wrong people for 12 years. Then in a moment of opportunity, I happened to be in the right place at the right time with the right person to ask the right question. Anyone could have done it. Are you asking the right questions?

Opportunity is in asking the right questions of the right people. Who are the right people in the scattered times you're living? What is your proximity to them? What can you do about it? Are you curious enough to break the glass ceiling in your brand of thinking? God's investment in you is worth the effort to live curious and push the limits. Traveling through your life is a no brainer. So is asking questions. So is doing exploits that move the dial beyond your normal hesitations. Anyone can be a tourist. But being a traveler? Ah, that's … well … that's everything the Opportunity Factor is about.

Now what? Identify your challenge. Explore your options. Then travel beyond the echoes of your past restrictions. Intentionally stretch into the transitions that will transform you. In this next section we'll focus on the disciplines necessary to take on opportunities.

FIGHTING THROUGH THE HIGHS AND LOWS OF TRANSITIONS

Remember when the first disciples were following Jesus from a distance, and He turned to them and asked: 'What do you want?' In all times, especially in scattered times, we need to decide what we want. That includes what we want out of the opportunities we are seeing, seizing, and navigating.

When teaching our church's internship in Canada, I came up with what I call

THE FOUR H.U.G.E. QUESTIONS
1. **WHAT ARE YOU HUNGRY FOR?**
2. **WHERE IS YOUR UNDERSTANDING LIMITED?**
3. **WHERE IS THE GRACE OF GOD THE STRONGEST?**
4. **WHAT ARE YOUR EXPECTATIONS AND WHY?**

WHAT ARE YOU HUNGRY FOR?
Hunger refers to a lack of nourishment. So, lets me reword that question: What nourishes you? What is the taste of life that you're missing? What makes you sense that something is lacking in your life? Where do you sense an incompleteness? What is it that you

once tasted that now eludes you? Natural hunger changes our outward appearance because something is missing on the inside of us. Spiritual hunger is more potent. It affects how we live inwardly and outwardly. It affects how we think.

Hungry, Jesus sent His disciples into town for food in the Gospel account of John 4:4-26. But when they came back from town, Jesus wasn't hungry! He had been hungry, but something happened while the disciples were in town. Jesus invested Himself in a conversation with a woman at the well. That conversation nurtured Him because it was His Father's will to encourage and reach people. The teacher in Him asked her the right questions and helped her discover the right answers that her life needed. Although exhausted from His day, He found nourishment in His conversation with a Samaritan. A Samaritan? Really? Yes, Jesus was often nourished outside the box of the societal norms of His day. Jews weren't supposed to talk with Samaritans, especially women. Jesus was a bit unpredictable. We should be, as well. Travelers are!

Here's the key to pushing through the opportunities in front of us.

Stay focused on what nourishes you. Never allow the roadblock of exhaustion to detour you from where you get your nourishment. There is always busy work to be done in opportunities, especially in scattered times. But our strength doesn't come from our *to do list*. Strength comes from the Lord. Strength comes from what nourishes us. Make a note of it.

Recognize what nourishes you. In the decades that followed graduate school, I was in constant production mode. Writing scripts, designing sets and lighting and building a team of actors to bring productions to life consumed my calendar. But what really nourished me were the rehearsals. In rehearsals, I worked to pull out of novice actors the abilities that they had never developed. As a director, one of the key skills is to always ask questions. Questions like *why does a character say this and not that? What is the subtext that motivates a character to say the words they say?* The *why* behind every word in a script uncovers the character's motive and gives the actor clarity. Clarity nourishes. As director, I always worked to create moments of impact that would nourish the audience. That magic came through in rehearsals. That's also the magic behind the scenes in our life where God works His magic! We have to keep asking ourselves 'what are we hungry for'? Knowing that, creates a Geiger counter type focus for what nourishes us.

Why is discovering the 'why' important? We have to live with an inward drive to satisfy what nourishes us, so that we are free to nourish others.

WHERE IS YOUR UNDERSTANDING LIMITED?

The opportunities we take on will inevitably require knowing where our understanding is lacking. Pat answers on how to resolve the empty places in the process of an opportunity only fill the gap for a moment. Living beyond our pat answers requires searching for something more, something fresh.

In the opportunity of a lifetime, there are gaps in our understanding but also pressures to settle for less. That pressure brings us to a point of going with what we already know or with our *best practices*, as we say in the business world. I understand there are *best practices* that keep working, but my point is this: **Relying on proven transactions from past experiences adds nothing to our arsenal of fresh understanding.** For me, settling is unsettling. The vacuum that needs to be filled is that place where our limited understanding stands wanting.

You could look for answers before you have questions. You could become a pusher of ideas. What if you read an hour a day? What if you read a variety of books that disturb you and challenge your routine vocabulary. Imagine searching for phrases and quotes to upgrade your conversations and hanging out with those who do the same. When you do, you'll become well aware that in some areas, you've been living your life seeing through a glass darkly. Realize that you could purpose to face the light of new adventures that would surpass your past limitations. Dare to become a committed Traveler. Now to the third question:

WHERE IS THE GRACE OF GOD THE STRONGEST?

The grace of God is routinely the strongest in our gift areas and uniqueness. It is more important to exercise our strengths than our weakness. Where grace flows, we excel. Leaning humbly into our strength areas lifts us to explore what we wouldn't otherwise notice. Grace empowers us to challenge ourselves and grow.

As I mentioned before, where our strengths are, we have a bias. The sufficiency of God's grace grows when we exercise them. I have a bias for leadership. Whenever I step into a situation that is disorganized and people seem scattered, my bias for leading takes charge if it is welcomed to do so. It is fulfilling to use our strengths wherever needed. Grace prompts us to lean in and make a difference.

WHAT ARE YOUR EXPECTATIONS AND WHY?

We base our expectations on where our hunger is. Even when our understanding is limited. Why? Because this is necessary to live what God is doing in our lives. Love His challenges because they move you forward. But there is something much more profound in answering these three questions.

They keep me in God's greatest initiative for my life. His greatest initiative remains forever in His desire to love on me. His love for me is at the heart of every defining moment of my life. Think about this: Jesus died to love on us. In fact, He died because His Father so loved the world that He...*you know the rest and you know it's true.*

When we allow God to love on us, His love transcends all the answers we seek. His love awakens us to His compassion. God wants to love us. We go to Africa or into ministry because He loves us, and we love Him back. When we allow Him to love on us until everything around us 'draws strangely dim,' it's a defining moment. Nothing else matters in that moment but Him. From that moment forward, scattered times don't matter. Difficulties in our challenging opportunities do not matter. Our personal world revolves best around Him loving on us and us responding to His love. In the greatest opportunities, we must gravitate back to Him loving on us.

Dearly loved children take chances to try new things. They travel into new adventures. By faith, dearly loved children find ways to please God not to earn His love, but because they already have and know His love. Perhaps that's what Jesus was really doing in the quiet nights with His Father. How could Jesus love the world He was plopped down into 2,000 ago unless He grew daily in defining moments of His Father's love. His Father's love poured out of Him into those standing before Him.

We don't survive or exceed in scattered times because we out maneuver obstacles thrown our way. We are summoned to time with God, not to survive but to thrive in our relationship with Him. On the grand scale of life, that's what matters the most. Time with Him is a game changer in scattered times. Opportunities demand it.

Our expectations, if anchored firmly in Him loving on us, will keep us nourished and focused. In His love opportunity makes more sense, even in scattered times. His love should be what we hunger for because from that starting place, His grace grows, our need is supplied, and our expectations rise. Now let's turn our focus to the unexpected.

UNEXPECTED TIMES

The unexpected is bound to happen. Somewhere in our busyness, we'll probably run out of gas. Resources will run out. Shipments will not come in. People will let us down. There will be obstacles shouting louder than the benefits. This is where healthy daily habits matter the most.

Everyday connect with your values and the options that support them. Without the clarity of our values, we will team up with partners contrary to them. Our patience in scattered times must match our opportunity in parallel. A former Prime Minister of the United Kingdom defined genius as **'prolonged patience'**! When the unexpected brings trouble our way, don't allow the trouble to distract you from thinking in the context of the bigger picture. Extend prolonged patience.

What we curse becomes our focus. Don't go there. Don't empower your setbacks to distract you from the main thing. Transitional toughness requires toughness that only grace can build. God's intervention is part of the plan. Don't stop one question short of His intervention. Keep Godly directions activated by stirring yourself up. Remember, beyond the deadline or opportunity in any transition, the takeaway is always a character issue.

We have to tap into the fragments of the thoughts that prevail. Understand that God's will takes time to grow on us. We have to see His intentions free from our negative expectations. It takes time to connect dots. Sometimes they are like herding cats! Jesus processed dots of information and revelation that surfaced before their activation time. He turned them over and over in His mind until they gelled for the moment needed. It matters that we turn our thoughts over and over without forcing their implementation before it's time for them to do so.

One more time, do you really live believing that:

God is passionately invested in us becoming someone we could never be without His directions and intervention.

Isn't that always the question?

5

THE TESTING PRINCIPLE

*It's not the load that breaks you
down, it's the way you carry it.*
—*C. S. Lewis*

*…when it seems as though you are facing nothing
but difficulties, see it as an invaluable opportunity to
experience the greatest joy that you can! <u>For you know
that when your faith is tested it stirs up power within
you to endure all things.</u> And then as your endurance
grows even stronger it will release perfection into every
part of your being until there is nothing missing and
nothing lacking.*

JAMES 1:2-4

An accomplished minister recently told me: "I like predictability;
I don't like change." His honesty reveals why challenging times are
difficult. As we grow in life, we tend to become stiff, unbendable,
and rigid. Change is unwelcome. The gravitational pull of our 'best
practices' prevents us from altering our framework to make room

for change. Within a familiar framework, all of life's puzzle pieces fit nicely. When life brings us a new puzzle piece, we don't know what to do with it.

Testing is a natural process in our spiritual walk. To more than survive such times, we have to constantly shift the conversation in our head. We can't allow our thinking to fall into panic and cave. We have to maintain a conversation in our heart and mind that spiritually toughens us up for the level of faith required. We can't fake it until we make it! We have to shift the conversation in our head, not just talk about it.

In scattered times, the mind game we're thrown into is complicated. There are multiple distractions attacking our normal mindset because our normal mindset isn't tough enough. Normal can't endure the moments that threaten normal! *Run of the mill* mindsets lack the toughness and level of thinking required in those times. Our spiritual instincts know it. Our spiritual instincts alert us, not to panic us, but to focus us on God's way of escape. His escape route is packed with more than it takes in the moment because He is building us for tomorrow. Toughness comes packaged differently than we expect. It always does.

Juggling daily life in troubling times becomes the difference between running a race on a well paved track and running one through the roughness of a terrain carpeted with mud and rocks. It's a hardcore walk of faith. Our thought processing in such times teeters back and forth between what used to be and what is. It is a stressful time and pretending it's not, won't make it go away. In scattered times, we're not given the luxury of being isolated from what's challenging us in the present in order to deal with the past. Testing may keep those reruns from our past playing while a whole new series of developments run simultaneously.

A sudden shift in our perspective is needed. But that shift can feel threatening by every remembrance of our shattered past. Already drained of the familiar, our mental security blanket is frayed. When yesterday's resources seem scattered beyond recognition, we have to fight off falling prey to the victim mentality we once condemned in others. This is reality slapping us in the face. Drained of yesterday's support resources, we have to fight through.

Picture with me a seed packet picked up by a customer in a garden center. The customer automatically shakes the packet. If you're one of the seeds trapped inside the sealed packet, what are you thinking? If that customer doesn't buy into you, you may never get out! You may subtly know that your buddies in the seed packet are your 'familiar.' If you are bought and get scattered, how will you keep in touch? You won't. Life outside your familiar packet will be 'unfamiliar'! Your out-of-the-packet experience will find you in soil you didn't choose. Outside conditions will vary. You need the right soil to grow and you know it. Or maybe you don't! Maybe the new owner of the packets knows what you need better than you do. Will they know where you've come from? Much of your life as a scattered seed depends on fitting into the soil where you're planted. It may not be your soil choice. Get the picture? In the farming culture that James knew, his description was a graphic reminder of what had happened to his persecuted friends. Yet, he saw their new ground differently.

Those scattered because of religious persecution and relocated to foreign lands did not choose this. They felt scattered, but not just geographically. They were persecuted for living a faith radically different from those of the familiar brands of the religions around them. They were scattered emotionally and mentally, as well. Fleeing their homeland had pushed every button. The sudden urgency to escape with their lives and meager possessions from their familiar *packet* had pushed them through the motions of a movement not of their own making. Never forget that Christianity is a movement. Movements move. Ultimately, these scattered believers would play a major part in spreading the Gospel throughout the known world. But first they would be the ones spread. They had been scattered and torn from all that had been familiar. This is the reality of the Testing Factor! Your experience probably pales in comparison to theirs, but in James' letter, there's a lot we can leverage for what we're going through in scattered times.

What leaves us feeling scattered? When our familiar becomes unfamiliar, we find ourselves transitioning to a new familiar. We have to cross what I call The Bridge of the Unfamiliar. This bridge will take us to a new familiar. In transition, it may not feel fair. Sometimes it's not.

COURAGE IS TESTED

Those scattered by religious persecution 2,000 years ago may have thought 'this is not what I signed up for'! Giving their life to Jesus came without a warning label that said: 'You will be tested!' However, even on the eve of the crucifixion, Jesus warned His followers that they would be tested, even scattered. Here's Jesus' message:

> *Jesus replied, Now you finally believe in me. And the time has come when you will all be scattered, and each one of you will go your own way, leaving me alone! Yet I am never alone, for the Father is always with me. And everything I've taught you is so that the peace which is in me will be in you and will give you great confidence as you rest in me. For in this unbelieving world you will experience trouble and sorrows, but you must be courageous, for I have conquered the world!*
> JOHN 16:31-33

Courage comes with a test. God's power within us is a treasure to be explored through real life experiences. We will be tested. The easy life requires no courage. Paul's defining moments came through testing. His life gained traction through physical and mental challenges packaged within His calling. It was almost like hard times chased him down for a fight. In his second letter to the Corinthians he writes:

> *We are like common clay jars that carry this glorious treasure within, so that the extraordinary overflow of power will be seen as God's, not ours. Though we experience every kind of pressure, we're not crushed. At times we don't know what to do, but quitting is not an option. We are persecuted by others, but God has not forsaken us. We may be knocked down, but not out. We continually share in the death of Jesus in our own bodies so that the resurrection life of Jesus will be revealed through our humanity.*
>
> II CORINTHIANS 4:7-10

THE COD FISH STORY

Perhaps you've heard this story before, but it exemplifies the point and value of testing.

At the turn of the century, the railroad made possible shipping goods from the east coast to the west coast of the United States. Once anyone from the west tasted the delicacies on the east coast, they wanted access to them back home. One of those delicacies was cod fish! Cod was a tasty delicacy in the day and in great demand like salmon is today. There was only one problem: getting cod fish all the way across the country with the freshness that had made it such a hit on the east coast. First, they tried to freeze the fish and send them by rail. That was a fast solution but when thawed out and cooked on the west coast, the cod were mushy and tasteless. Their lack of freshness caused them to lose their desired flavor. Frozen fish was out.

Some tenacious person came up with the idea of shipping the fish alive. That required creating giant aquariums in railroad cars! Again, when they arrived alive and were prepared, they were still mushy and without the fresh flavor desired.

Further study uncovered the natural enemy of cod fish. Catfish! So, they added catfish to the tanks to chase the cod! Why? Because by adding their enemy, the catfish, to the tanks, everything changed. Their freshness was maintained in the chase. Remove the chase, and the cod became mushy and tasteless versions of themselves. It was the challenge of the chase that had been missing. The chase was needed to keep them fresh!

The same is true for us. The most vivacious and courageous believers are kept fresh by the chase. It is the trying of our faith that stirs up power, and stirred power keeps us fresh. Freshness requires the chase. That's part of the test! No chase, no freshness! No challenge, no freshness. Testing keeps us fresh. No test, and we too become a mushy and tasteless version of ourselves.

ENDURING THE TEST

Remember James 1:3? ***For you know that when your faith is tested it stirs up power within you to endure all things.*** Endurance requires power, but not static power, stirred power. Paul reminded Timothy to stir up the gift of God that was in him. Why? Because in Timothy's case, timidity and fear were compromising his calling. Paul reminded him that God's gift was the gift of power, love, and a sound mind. No stirring, no freshness.

What does it take to keep yourself stirred? What does it take to keep you tasty? When are you the most alive and most powerful? I suspect there is something significant that God desires to release within us when we are being chased! Jesus lived in the chase. Paul lived in the chase. Those who changed the world lived in the chase. The same is true for us today.

Isn't it the update of God's presence that keeps us fresh? Now you're probably thinking - *I'd rather just enjoy the ride without the 'catfish.'* I understand, but those hungry for God need your freshness. They need the full-flavored edition of the treasure God has put in you. Paul lived the fresh version of why God called him. From the moment of his conversion God was upfront with him, even blunt! Consider the message God gave Ananias to give to Paul at the outset of his conversion:

> *The Lord Yahweh answered him, "Arise and go I have chosen this man to be my special messenger. He will be brought before kings, before many nations and before the Jewish people to give them the revelation of who I am. And I will show him how much he is destined to suffer because of his passion for me.*
>
> ACTS 9:15-16

I'm not saying go out and create a test. I'm saying that when you are really tested, see it as an invaluable opportunity. Toughen up when your faith is tested. Know that testing stirs up power in you to endure. Know also that as your endurance level grows, you'll become more and more the character of Christ that our world needs. There are people around you that need you to be the fresh version of God's treasure in you. Are you up to the chase?

Since difficult times find most of us unprepared and scattered, James' concept of maturity includes experiencing the greatest joy because of something we know. That something is a knowledge of how God comes to our rescue when life throws us off balance. Only when the power of God inside of us is greater than the pressure of life outside of us can we keep it together.

Spiritual maturity is born through perseverance in difficult times. Difficult times test what we really believe. Trying times puts our faith on trial. James knows what scattered means because he's been there. So had Paul. The apostles Paul and James were in agreement. Their concepts of what makes one spiritually mature align. What James writes in the opening of his letter, Paul also writes to Roman believers going through similar times.

Here are Paul's words:

> *But that's not all! Even in times of trouble we have a joyful confidence, knowing that our pressures will develop in us patient endurance. And patient endurance will refine our character, and proven character leads us back to hope.*
>
> ROMANS 5:3-4

CHARACTER

Invaluable opportunities focus on refining our character. Why? Variableness in our character causes our faith to come up short. It is clear in James' letter that the trying times he's writing about do not originate from God. James makes this point crystal clear in verses 13-14. While he declares trying times as not of God's doing, he declares that the redemptive and refining opportunities in those times are from God. In other words, regardless of what life throws at us, God orchestrates invaluable opportunities to refine our character. That may be where confusion comes. Paul adds that refined character leads us back to hope. What gets lost in the shuffle of scattered times? Hope! What is gained by living Paul and James' way? Hope.

When Paul writes about having a joyful confidence or James writes about experiencing the greatest joy, they are not telling us to rejoice because times are tough. They are admonishing us to rejoice in what God purposes to do in spite of our tough times. They know that the expected outcome of adverse circumstances includes two things. First, when our faith is tried, God's power manifests itself in us. Secondly, when His power runs its course, our endurance extends, and our character matures. His purpose is to toughen us up to the point that difficulties no longer throw us off course.

I know what you're thinking. Perhaps it's the devil's doing. Maybe. I know that you know what Jesus tells us about the thief.

> *The thief has only one thing in mind – he wants to steal, slaughter, and destroy.*
>
> JOHN 10:10

Why do we always want to blame everything on the devil? What good does that do? Yes, the devil causes havoc in our lives, but he's not the only one. In James' letter, he doesn't put the emphasis on the devil. Instead, he focuses on challenging those who are scattered. In his letter, he confronts their thinking, wisdom, conversations, love for others, and much more. In our society, James' letter comes without pity! He knows that people in troubling times need a challenge, not pity. Compassion? Yes. Pity? No. A challenge? Yes!

Certainly, God's promises and blessings are ours. We should fight to live them. Yes, we should. What is also true is that we tend to get distracted. When things are going well, we pick up random trappings. When those are worldly trappings, they become weights and distractions. Worldly trappings may include mindsets contrary to God's wisdom. When we tolerate trappings as add-ons, we create avenues of distraction. Then, our point of view becomes fuzzy. We lose our Kingdom focus. Mentally, emotionally, and spiritually we become scattered. This reality is at the heart of James' letter. He offers a compassionate rebuke.

Here's what I've learned.

In scattered times, the Holy Spirit jumps on every opportunity to make character and course corrections. His purpose is to reorient us. God wants to tweak our character. He wants us to see teachable moments as treasures in unfamiliar times. Old ways of seeing the changes and challenges life throws at us have to be reviewed. They need to be updated and made relevant for the purposes of God. We have to live in *now*, not yesterday. God takes advantage of the challenges that trying times cause to refocus and stretch us!

What's your heart fastened to? Famous verses we quote from Paul's letter to the Philippians coincide with James' challenge to scattered people. Paul writes from his own experience. His focus in trying times gives us the leverage needed to meet James' challenges. Check out Philippians 3:12-14:

> *I admit that I haven't yet acquired the absolute fullness that I'm pursuing, but I run with passion into his abundance so that I may reach the purpose that Jesus Christ has called me to fulfill and wants me to discover. I don't depend on my own strength to accomplish this, however, I do have one compelling focus: I forget all of the past as <u>I fasten my heart to the future instead.</u> I run straight for the divine invitation of reaching that Heavenly goal and gaining the victory-prize through the anointing of Jesus.*

Wow! Paul calls our attention to where we *fasten our heart*. Paul mastered fastening his heart to his future, not to his past. I know we may read this as Paul's effort to leave behind his horrible pre-conversion days of arresting and killing believers. But that's not what he says here. A closer read tells us where he has 'fastened his heart.' You may remember the same verse from a more familiar translation of the same scripture:

> *...Forgetting what is behind and straining toward what is ahead, I press on toward the goal to win the prize for which God has called me...*
>
> (PHILIPPIANS 3:12-14 NIV)

Where Paul fastened his heart is where he stretched forward. Is where you've fastened your heart forward? Backward? Paul's letter to the Philippians comes packed with exactly what we need in unfamiliar and trying times. It matters where we attach our hearts.

Life's a stretch, and stretching should bring us closer to Jesus. James writes later in the same letter: *Draw near to God and He will draw near to you* (James 4:8 (NIV)). When our way of processing life has become rigid, we need to stretch closer. Stretching narrows our focus to see and our listening to hear.

Realize that James' directives do not challenge any doctrinal beliefs. His direction and intervention casts no doubt on the reality of anyone's salvation. Neither does Paul's writing to the Philippians compromise their theology. Both of these New Testament writers, James and Paul, are just challenging where we've fastened our hearts. Why? Because our perspectives and mindsets are anchored to where our hearts are fastened. Stretching keeps us anchored and agile in our relationship with Jesus, even when life throws a curve.

- *Where do you need to be stretched?*
- *Where have you become rigid?*

- *Where do you attach your heart when life gets scattered?*

DAVID GOGGINS' STORY

In his book <u>Can't Hurt Me</u>, David Goggins tells of a time that caught him and everyone around him by surprise. His success as a Navy Seal and ultra-marathon, triathlon, and ultra-triathlon champion hardened his mind and body to take on any challenge. He had outgrown the abused, depressed, and limited version of his childhood. He had challenged everything head on for years. One day his body began to challenge back! He found himself unable to run, or walk even a mile. His body refused to be pushed. His vision literally blurred. He began to have trouble getting out of bed. His doctors searched for a solution but to no avail. He thought he was going to die. Talk about scattered – he was there.

One day, he reached his hand around his neck and felt a familiar knot at his neck's base. He realized it had grown larger than before. There were also two other knots above his hip flexors. He then had a flash back moment from his Navy Seal training of a session led by Joe Hippensteel. He had lectured on the value of stretching. Goggins had not been a fan. Hippensteel cautioned against the overuse and overdevelopment of muscles without the balance of flexibility exercises. Coggins had ignored the warning.

But at this point in his life, he suspected that Hippensteel was right. He wondered if stretching was the key to his recovery. He tried stretching only to find that stretching his muscles was like stretching steel cables. With his characteristic tenacity to tackle everything full throttle, he began stretching his way back to health. He initially found that his muscles were so locked up that his blood wasn't able to circulate. His muscles were like frozen steaks!

They couldn't inject a flow of blood, and that's why his body was shutting down.

Stretching became an obsession. Over time, the knot at the base of his neck began to shrink, as did the others. His energy level slowly returned. His health returned. His recovery instituted stretching as a forever part of his lifestyle. Hint. Hint. Stretching is life-giving.

When we become frozen in our routine mindsets and practices, we also limit how we see opportunities. We need to stretch, not just physically, but mentally and even spiritually. Otherwise, we become a mentally-immobile version of who God created us to be. Paul's lifestyle had always been a stretch. From his dramatic confrontation and conversion with the reality of Jesus Christ as Lord and Savior, he never stopped stretching. In the scattered and trying times of Paul's life, he learned not to live attached to his past. He practiced stretching forward spiritually. He attached his heart to the heart of Jesus and never looked back.

Paul went from evangelizing the world and teaching the revelation of who Jesus is to prison. In a prison cell he lived scattered and challenged. In those unfamiliar times he stretched forward. He searched for the invaluable opportunities hidden behind bars. He evangelized his guards. The Holy Spirit prompted him to write letters to the churches. A joyous adventure began. Power stirred. Endurance grew. His Godly character matured. In the environment of scattered times, Paul wrote more than half of the New Testament. Amazing what stretching can do!

Where do you need to stretch?

GIDEON'S STORY

In Judges 6-7, Gideon's story is a *scattered times* classic. Allow me to break his story into an acronymic play on his name. Acronyms make it easier to remember important information. I use them often. Here's how G.I.D.E.O.N. helps us remember his story in his winepress days:

G   GUILTY (Israel's cry for deliverance only left them feeling guilty and without hope)

I   INFERIOR (Gideon saw his tribe, his family, and himself as the least of the least)

D   DISAPPOINTED (He grew angry/disappointed in the God who didn't deliver them)

E   EMPTY (He grew up hiding from his enemies; his existence left him empty)

O   OVERWHELMED (Prospects for his future in light of his present overwhelmed him)

N   NON-COMBATIVE (No one else was fighting; he found no reason to do otherwise)

Gideon had sabotaged his life with low self-esteem and anger that dismissed God's presence. But, ultimately, he became a champion. From the moment he began to attach his heart to God's words from an angel, he began to progressively grow in eight major areas. Each area stretched him exponentially forward to become the champion of God's intentions.

8 C.H.A.M.P.I.O.N. GROWTH AREAS THAT STRETCHED GIDEON FORWARD:

(Definitions from Oxford Dictionary)

C   Curiosity – A desire to experience or learn something new

H   Hunger - A strong desire or craving that can't be shaken

A   Awareness - Knowledge or perception of a situation from God's point of view

M   Movement - A change or development decision in a resolute direction

P   Purpose - The reason for which something or someone exists

I   Identity - Being who or what a person or thing is from God's perspective

O   Obedience - Compliance to orders or submission to another's authority

N   Navigator - Director or explorer of a course or direction

All that Gideon had believed about himself before the confrontation and conversion of himself as God's champion created a hardened shell around him. In that hardness, faith was muffled by unanswered questions and anger. Fear was king. But when the angel of the Lord met him in the wine press, Gideon began to discover that God is not limited. God doesn't isolate Himself because of our inadequacies, history, or fears. God just goes on being God! When Israel called out to God, God called out to them.

GENE BRACK

Gideon's conversation with the angel revealed more than just his anger at God. Subliminally, it revealed a curiosity and hunger to understand God. Curiosity and hunger for God always stretches us forward. Threshing wheat couldn't stretch Gideon because he was hiding out in fear. He was misplaced and thought he might die in the winepress. Haven't we all? The angel told him 'you won't die here.' The angel's message was strategic. Gideon tore down his father's pagan altar and did so without fear that he would die there. His faith in what the angel told him gained traction.

Military tactics and strategies began flexing their muscles in Gideon. Without fear, he blew trumpets and called those cowering in the hills to respond to the battle cry in his heart. Perhaps even before the angel's words, Gideon had rehearsed military tactics in his mind. His purpose and calling to be a champion warrior had always been in him. But like most of us, Gideon hadn't owned what was instinctively in him because he lived blinded by what was around him. His 'least of them' identity had locked him into less.

Gideon's confidence in God eventually allowed him to reduce 32,000 followers down to 100. His stretch as a champion warrior climaxed not in war but as a spy in the enemy's camp. God's directive to sneak into the enemy's camp and hear what they were thinking transformed Gideon. He found that his enemy had grown paranoid that the God of the Israelites was about to attack them. Gideon's confidence and obedience to God's way of thinking instigated the navigational force that led his people to victory. As he came to believe God, he stretched forward into the corresponding actions that changed everything. So can we.

AS A CHAMPION OF GOD, GIDEON CAME TO BELIEVE THAT:

1. God was with him.
2. God's favor was on him.
3. God's power was in him.
4. God's victory was his victory.
5. God's plan was alive inside him.

It is far better to be confident and courageous in our own skin than to just be comfortable in it. Gideon became knowledgeable that God was working behind the scenes to assure his victory. Attaching his heart to that knowledge was climatic in Gideon's transformation. He became the champion needed in the scattered times he lived.

Gideon's life was a stretch but not until he changed the way he saw himself. When he did, he also changed where his heart had been attached. Faith replaced fear. For years, Gideon stretched away from God's intentions. In both stories, Goggins and Gideon had to focus on stretching their thinking beyond the framework of what had become their best practices. Both moved beyond their rigid way of thinking. Goggins and Gideon attached their hearts to a paradigm shift in what they believed to be true. So can we.

LEANING IS THE STARTING PLACE

Holding on to the promises of God by walking in them enriches our character and builds our spiritual toughness. This level of toughness doesn't grow out of thin air. This level of toughness grows in the chase. It's part of the process of growing in Christ. Testing requires toughness. Sometimes we have to grow in a crunch. Learning how to handle tough times is invaluable. When we tackle a difficult time, we have to find something to lean into. Let me dig a little more into Proverbs 3:5-6 to bring home this point.

Trust in the Lord with all your heart, and do not lean on your own understanding. In all your ways acknowledge him and he will make straight your paths.

(KJV)

Wherever we lean our thinking and trust, a path appears. What if we lean into fear and doubt? The principle holds true. There a path will appear. Lean into anger and the principle holds true. When we lean into committing everything to the Lord, a life-giving path appears. By appear, I'm not talking about magically or graphically written on a wall. The will of God grows on us. Let's go back to Proverbs 16:3. If we commit the work (the situation, problem, opportunity) to the Lord, he begins to establish (give us a foundation to stand on) our thinking. Establishment of the 'thinking' path takes time. Prolonged patience required. His thoughts grow on us; His relationship with us grows as well. But we have to find that starting place every time. God knows what's coming before it comes. Testing in school came after the class lectures or labs. So, it is with God. The breadcrumbs along the path where he leads us are not random. He is strategic. The Holy Spirit is as intentional about teaching us, guiding us, and fathering us before the test as He is during the test. Our focus needs to be consistent. Time in His Word prepares us. Testing alerts us to the Holy Spirit has been teaching us. Testing awakens us to connect the dots of where He has been taking our hearts. A mixture of thoughts that cause us to waver, leaves us unstable and dots disconnected.

Word of Caution: A mixture of thoughts grows when we're divided in our faith. Variableness in giving our all to the Lordship of Christ puts us on shifting sand when it comes to committing our work, problem, or situation to the Lord. A mixture of thoughts violates our trust and dilutes our faith. When we waver in committing our work to Him, we dislodge the stability He is endeavoring to establish in our thinking. It follows that whenever we lack the wisdom necessary, we should ask for it. And asking must be a solid ask, backed by consistent faith. Dig into James 1:5-8 again, and you'll see what the author is really saying to the scattered church.

The power to consistently believe that God is working out our thoughts is stirred by our consistency of faith. Our consistency is evidenced by where we consistently lean. When I lean on something, I trust it. I check it out, and then I lean. There are foundational truths from which I never waver. But in each new situation or challenge, leaning gives me a starting place.

Believing, leaning, and trusting is attractive to God. He's always ready. In fact, I've learned that He is already working things out before I start leaning. Leaning just tunes me in to what He has already purposed. He sees the testing coming before it comes to my attention. He is always working *backstage* in our lives. If we make leaning into His word part of our daily workout, we'll hear the cues for our next line of response. God is always our first responder.

JESUS' SPIRITUAL TOUGHNESS

Jesus' forty days in the wilderness was no picnic. From my knowledge of scriptures, Jesus had never before been in a wilderness with the devil! He recently had been tagged publicly by His Father as the son in 'whom He was well pleased!'

Spiritual toughness is not grown in the lab of controlled circumstances. Spiritual toughness is grown in the field. Toughness is not a matter of fairness nor is it a measure of inheritance. Jesus learned obedience through the things He suffered. (Hebrews 5:8). No one wants to sign up for suffering. Suffering is not appealing on its own. Jesus would eventually wrestle suffering to the ground and rise victoriously.

What should be most appealing to us is what we become on the other side of suffering. Who sees that coming? Scripture says Jesus returned from his earliest wilderness experience in the power of the Holy Spirit. We celebrate that thought in Jesus' life but celebrating doesn't toughen us up. Experiencing life in difficult or scattered times should transition us to a new understanding of toughness.

James knew what He was talking about in his letter to scattered believers. He was reminding them of something they knew but were not actively living. He was, in essence, commanding them to toughen up. Their lesson must become our lesson in scattered times. We learn from the following text that Jesus' lifetime on earth required spiritual toughness.

> *We look away from the natural realm and we fasten our gaze onto Jesus who birthed faith within us and who leads us forward into faith's perfection. His example is this: Because his heart was focused on the joy of knowing that you would be his, he endured the agony of the cross and conquered its humiliation, and now sits exalted at the right hand of the throne of God. So, consider carefully how Jesus faced such intense opposition from sinners who opposed their own souls, so that you won't become worn down and cave in under life's pressure.*
>
> HEBREWS 12:2-3

That's a download of truth that may take a little time to wrap our heads around. We have to rise above what our enemy leverages against us. The devil always hopes to wear us down to the point that we cave to pressures. Let's start by studying how Jesus grew in spiritual toughness.

Do you really think Jesus just waltzed into the crucifixion? Do you think Gethsemane was the first time he fought *caving in*? What do you think it means in Hebrews 4:15?

He understands humanity, for as a Man, our magnificent King-Priest was tempted in every way just as we are, and conquered sin.

He not only conquered sin; He conquered temptation! That would include times of being worn down, even scattered! Let's be real here. Jesus grew in His spiritual toughness, and so must we. Forty days in the wilderness took Him into an unfamiliar and intense time. The word 'wilderness' refers to a waste land, a desolate and solitary place. Emptied of all that was familiar, Jesus worked His way through the wilderness and the temptations that inhabited the testing He found there. Angels were withheld from ministering to Him until the devil left Him. But there's more.

The devil didn't even show up until Jesus was extremely weak and famished! Then, at the end of 40 days of fasting, the tempter came. Jesus was more than famished. He had lost the vigor of what daily sustenance would have provided. His body yearned for nourishment, but none would be provided until the devil left Him! Jesus was tempted. This was no Sunday School lesson. This was a season of being scrutinized and enticed and examined by the great tempter himself. Jesus was doing lab time in what could have left Him undone, except, He stood tough.

Scripture says that Jesus resisted. He backed the devil against the wall. Eventually, the devil left Him for a season. For a season? Yes, temptation and testing are for a season – they are not a life sentence. The testing season of our faith develops a spiritual toughness. Jesus returned in the power of the Holy Spirit, but before He returned in the Holy Spirit's strength, He had to stand tough. Toughness is not built in the easy times. Toughness takes us beyond what seems necessary in the moment. Why? In order to give us the momentum for the toughness needed for the seasons that follow. Toughness builds when we stand by faith in God's Word. His Word strengthens us. Our prolonged patience in standing toughens us. It is possible to feel scattered and not even flinch, but we have to toughen up to live there.

Toughness grows as we resist Satan's brute force of intimidation. To the hungry, Satan offers a way to be fed. Jesus rejected Satan's offer. Even in the early days of Jesus' ministry, He knew where His nourishment came from. His nourishment came from doing His Father's will. Nothing else satisfied Him. He stood tough against the tempter's enticement to turn stones into bread. His spiritual toughness was growing.

Jesus' resistance against temptation was not a matter of motivation. Motivation proves itself thin in times of testing. Testing comes back to what we really know, not to what we feel. Review James' charge to the scattered believers: *For you know that when your faith is tested it stirs up power within you to endure all things. And then as your endurance grows even stronger it will release perfection into every part of your being until there is nothing missing and nothing lacking.*

The expectancy of power stirred in the tested becomes the catalyst for endurance. James admonishes scattered people to see their moment of testing as the opportunity to experience the greatest joy. Such joy is not based on our personal toughness to survive. The joy he is referring to is God's supernatural presence and power working mightily within us. Our toughness manifests at the same time.

Toughness is not about our track record, personality, or likability. Toughness does not result from playing the comparison game where we compare ourselves among ourselves. The comparison game is convoluted and a slippery slope to nowhere. The comparison game is a tactic of Satan to distract us.

Faux spirituality and superiority lash out at those around us who aren't in the battle we're in. Faux is faux. James tells us that what we need 'face in the mirror' time. He speaks of a two-way mirror. First, we look into the mirror of God's Word. Secondly, we look at ourselves in comparison to God's Word. We need to talk bluntly to the version of us staring back. We need to declare the Word of God to ourselves. We need to have a healthy life-giving talk with ourselves.

This holds valuable in times scattered and not scattered. I've learned to look deeper into the Word of God, especially in the famous verses that we so often quote. There is no spiritual toughness outside of examining the Word of God. Toughness makes calculating moves to line up with the Word in reflective times. I find it a best practice to not only read the Word but to allow the Word to read me! Read slowly through the following verses:

> *Don't just listen to the Word of Truth and not respond to it, for that is the essence of self-deception. So always let His Word become like poetry written and fulfilled by our life! If you listen to the Word and don't live out the message you hear, you become like the person who looks in the mirror of the Word to discover the reflection of his face in the beginning. You perceive how God sees you in the mirror of the Word, but then you go out and forget your divine origin.*
>
> *But those who set their gaze deeply into the perfecting law of liberty are fascinated by and respond to the truth they hear and are strengthened by it - they experience God's blessing in all that they do!*
>
> JAMES 1:22-25

If we allow the Word of God to read us, we begin to see ourselves as we really are in the moment of our testing. We receive from the truth of God's word the energy to toughen ourselves up in line with what the Word reveals. We aren't expected to do this alone. It's a team venture with the Holy Spirit. His purpose is to father us through this life, but we have to be open to Him fathering us. He coaches us in line with the Word of God in reference to where we really are. But He also fathers us in reference to where we need to go.

We have to confront ourselves with His Truth. We have to take a good look at ourselves and make the adjustments as we go. We don't have the luxury of waiting for better times in which to make those adjustments. They must be made in the life of the time we're living. There are few times more perfect than scattered times to take a second look at ourselves. A relationship with Jesus has to matter to the point that we invite Him into our mirror! We should welcome and necessitate His intervention. It's our expected responsibility.

Concerning the Word of God, the writer of Hebrews further clarifies this point. Slowly read through the following verses, then let's talk some more.

> *For we have the living Word of God, which is full of energy, like a two-mouthed sword. It will even penetrate to the very core of our being where soul and spirit, bone and marrow meet! It interprets and reveals the true thoughts and secret motives of our hearts. There is not one person who can hide their thoughts from God, for nothing that we do remains a secret, and nothing created is concealed, but everything is exposed and defenseless before his eyes, to whom we must render an account.*
> HEBREWS 4:12-13

The note in the Passion Bible Translation concerning verse 12 remarks that **'God's word has the ability to uncover our hidden aspects and make them known.'** This is the turning point in the perspective in trying times. The uncovering of what's really going on in our mental processing in trying times, is of spiritual consequence. 'Face in the mirror' times are not efforts of the Holy Spirit to condemn us. 'Face in the mirror' times with the Holy Spirit are purposed to deepen our relationship with Jesus. We should intentionally initiate such times. Our transparency with the Holy Spirit should prove invigorating. The energy of His correction, direction, and intervention is transformational.

> *And then as your endurance grows even stronger it will release perfection into every part of your being until there is nothing missing and nothing lacking.*
>
> JAMES 1:4

The Passion Bible Translation says 'endurance,' the King James says 'patience'. Either way endurance and patience are released when we choose to totally rely on God. The strength of endurance and patience releases a measure of 'perfection' or maturity that only God's wisdom can provide. Thus, in the verse that follows, James instructs scattered people who lack wisdom to ask for it. Good News: We aren't limited to the wisdom we know so far. God's wisdom is ours for the asking. As He establishes His thoughts in our thinking, wisdom advances. Wholeness in our character is God's target in trying times. Paul writes to the Roman believers assuring them that God desires to conform them to the likeness of His Son.

> *For he knew all about us before we were born and he destined us from the beginning* **to share the likeness of his Son.**
>
> ROMANS 8:29

Wholeness of character is our greatest need in scattered times. We know that we have some missing pieces. God knows what they are and how to integrate them in our life. Conforming us to the likeness of Jesus is the ongoing work of the Holy Spirit. The 'joy of the Lord' is typically not our strength in scattered times. We should notice when we're coming up joy-short! The tests of our lifetime is on-going. Difficulties we go through may test every fiber of our being.

6

THE CHARACTER TESTING PRINCIPLE

How you leave one place determines
how you enter the next place.
— *Ed Cole*

Since graduate school, I've leaned heavily on this scripture in Proverbs 16:3 (KJV): **Commit thy works unto the Lord, and thy thoughts will be established.** I continue to lean into this scripture because it keeps me open to a freshness in my relationship with Jesus. That freshness prevents panic whenever life throws me a curve. This truth began quietly in graduate school. It has empowered me in the trying times of death and betrayal, as well.

I acted on this promise before I knew it was a scripture. For example, in graduate school, I majored in set and lighting design. Every week I was responsible for bringing to class a perspective in color of a set design for a different play. That required, of course, reading dozens of plays and technically drawing the design and then coloring it. In the process, I realized I was clueless in the color realm. The color scheme was my challenge. It kept me in the chase week after week.

Because I grew up in a home that was literally off-white, my concept of color was lacking. I could design the set, but I couldn't color it. My process for solving this challenge was to select a play, sketch a set design, and then commit the final results to the Lord. That didn't mean that I was sitting around waiting for God to appear with a color pallet. Here's what I learned.

At the point of completing the uncolored set design, I would leave the drawing board (yes, this was before computers), and JoAn and I would go to the mall. In the mall I studied every window display for color and texture. I became color conscious. As I did, I became texture conscious, as well. I absorbed them both. The proportions of objects playing off other objects in the window would catch my eye. I critiqued each window as to what was pleasing to the eye and what was not. Also, I learned what would lend itself to comedies verses tragedies. My creativity grew from these walks in the mall. But, first, I had to lean into this process by faith. Uncolored set designs chased me. I had to fold the creative process into my way of thinking. Once I leaned in far enough, the color pallet became a reality. It was like I chased it until it chased me back.

> *Trust in the Lord with all your heart; and lean not to your own understanding; in all your ways submit to him, and he will make your paths straight.*
> PROVERBS 3:5-6 (NIV)

Here's a visual of this Proverb. Picture an extension ladder. An extension ladder has to be leaned against something to be useful. Wherever we lean an extension ladder, a path appears! We follow the steps and go up the ladder to a desired destination. Committing our work to the Lord leans our trust into Him. Wherever we lean our trust in Him, a path appears, God's truth is always chasing us so he can direct our paths.

Committing our work to the Lord and allowing Him to establish our thoughts doesn't mean that we sit in a quiet place and wait for the Lord to show up. Usually, we have to keep doing life in the midst of working through difficulties. Time doesn't stand still. But as I worked through these principles in graduate school, my trust in God's ability grew. The promises of God are 'yes and amen' in Christ. (II Corinthians 1:20) Leaning into a promise in God's word that meets our need creates a path for His provision. Why? Because it creates a path for our faith to follow!

In graduate school, even before knowing that verse in Proverbs 16, my faith grew each week in the anticipation of a finished product. I was in partnership with Him and He with me. Our relationship was a team endeavor. I became resilient in this process in project after project.

I began to expect great joy in the final product before there was a final product. Learning to rely on God in this practical realm developed a process in my relationship with Him. That process has continued to prove itself as valuable truth. Whether writing a book, preparing a talk, or acclimating to a new adventure, these verses of wisdom in Proverbs hold true. Today, I can rejoice in trying times because I know there is power that arises within me when I do. There's always a test, but God is faithful to prep us for the chase beforehand. We can live following through where his Spirit leads us before the test. But even if sometimes the test catches us off guard, it never catches God off guard.

JAMES MICHAEL & THE UNEXPECTED

In 1979, we were expecting our third child. Everyone was excited. Ladies in the church had given us a beautiful Jenny Lynn crib. Everything was ready. But in the early hours of December 5, tragedy struck. Our third child was born dead. It sent shock waves through our faith.

I left the hospital to go tell the older two children what had happened. I had no words. On the drive to where they were waiting, I began a conversation with God. It wasn't the 'why did this happen' conversation, but the 'what now' conversation. Because of Proverbs 16:3 and Proverbs 3:5-6, committing the work of this moment to the Lord was as natural as committing the need for color on a set design. This process had become so engrained in my thinking that it was an easy shift from the emotion of the tragedy to the only way forward that I knew.

Recalling lyrics from an Imperial concert song, I began to worship the Lord for who He was. Their song lyrics were: 'Praise the Lord, He can work through those who praise him.' That was my starting place. Proverbs 16:3 was my 'go to' place. In that moment, the Holy Spirit brought to my mind the scripture in Isaiah 53:4, which says that 'He bore our griefs and carried our sorrows.' Realizing that God did not create us to bear grief or carry sorrow awoke a strength in me, and I began to shift the situation over to Him. In the quietness of my drive that morning, I gave him my grief. I knew that in the moment we would grieve, but in the momentum of moving forward, grief would pass.

And that is what happened. JoAn and I both moved forward, not just for our own sakes, but for the sake of those around us in the family and church we loved. God proved himself strong in us. That day and those that followed assured us that wherever we leaned our faith, a path would appear! In season after season, this has proven true. We continue to walk in this truth today. Certainly, it was the grace of God that carried us through James Michael's death. But that grace was the same grace developed by walking the mall for color schemes in set design. Learning grace learned several years before became the needed power stirred within me at our son's death. Grace chases after us. David wrote in Psalm 23 (KJ): 'surely goodness and mercy follows after me all the days of my life'. Today the memory of James Michael serves as a vivid reminder of God's faithfulness in trying times.

THE BATTLE OF 1994

Initially, it wasn't faith that stirred our hearts in what we call the Battle of 1994. Our hearts had been robbed of all that had been familiar for more than 20 years.

What happened? In short, the pastor I had worked with for more than a decade called me into his office on the Saturday before Christmas in 1993. He told me that he was leaving our church to begin a traveling ministry. Because we had both come on staff at the same time, he convincingly told me that since he was resigning, I should too! Then came the lie that I fell for against all logic. He told me the new pastor coming in did not want me and neither did the church board. His sinister mandate left me speechless. He would resign for both of us at the same time.

Only if you've been in the presence of someone who could convince you that the sky was green with orange polka dots, can you understand how I fell for his deception. Why did I believe I had to resign? This man had the ability to tell you anything, no matter how illogical, and you would believe it. His trickery went deeper than this moment in his office. Within a week, he was at my house wanting to know where I was planning to go! He, obviously, wanted my resignation to come across as my decision. He could spin it better, that way. But I had no direction. A week wasn't long enough to wrap my head around what was happening, much less the ramifications of what moving would entail.

During the week following our resignations, each board member met with me and asked the same question: 'Was your resignation your idea or his'? 'It was his,' I replied honestly each time. As I relayed what I had been told on that Saturday morning before Christmas, each of us knew that all of us had been lied to. The web of deceit ran deeper than anyone imagined.

The new pastor was already on his way from the western U. S. It was a done deal. I believed that to fight the lie that had been dumped on us would have caused confusion and division among the people I deeply loved.

The good news was that the new pastor allowed me to work with him until I could find another ministry. Several months later, in my final week with him, he told me that everything he had been told by the previous pastor was a lie. I never knew what the former pastor had told him. I'm grateful I never had to deal with that on top of what was to become the most scattered time of our lives.

During the months between December and my departure in April, my wife and I walked in love among the several hundred people that we had faithfully served.

No one wanted us to leave. We were loved and appreciated. Deep inside, we believed we had to walk carefully through this transition. It was a test, but it was nothing compared to the test that followed our departure.

How you leave one situation determines how you enter the next one.

ED COLE

A church in Davenport, Iowa offered me a position as youth pastor. Iowa is more than a thousand miles from where we had gone to college and served churches in Mississippi and Alabama. But their offer was the only choice I had. I moved myself there shortly after Easter that year, and the family followed as soon as school was out in June. That's when the test became real.

We weren't tough enough. We hadn't healed enough. The deception of our former pastor ran like television reruns in our mind. We felt torn away from relationships we had built for more than 20 years. On top of that was the fact that I had spent the last decade teaching and ministering to adults. Overnight, I found myself standing in a large room that would hold over a hundred youth but had only a handful of teenagers. They were the remnant of whatever went before me.

The move was not just about JoAn and I. The move was also about our five children. They too had been uprooted from their friends. Our oldest two were out of high school. The youngest three were ages 5 to 12 years. JoAn took a night shift job to help us meet the financial demands of living in Iowa winters. It was a brutal transition on multiple levels.

We were brought face to face with a totally different culture. Davenport is on the shorelines of the Mississippi River. The climate was brutally cold in the winter, and winter was not limited to mere freezing as we had known it. Think of wind chill of forty below zero, and you're close. The population of the town we moved from in Mississippi was a mere 30,000. The greater Davenport area, known as the Quad Cities, was nearly 400,000!

Our hearts were broken emotionally. We were stunned spiritually. We were financially strapped. We purchased a home that summer, only weeks before the pastor of the church resigned! The Davenport church board put my brother up to become the new lead pastor. He had served as Associate Pastor there and was well liked. But he missed becoming pastor by one vote. He and his family moved away after Christmas that year. All the reasons we had moved there were gone by year's end. We felt crushed and scattered. Trying to let go of the past and take hold of the present was like straddling life by wearing two roller skates going in opposite directions.

I cried for months and months. So did JoAn. We were broken in so many places. Some of the youth were vocal about not wanting us there. I came out one night after our youth service to find someone had written in the dust on the window of our car: 'Go back to Mississippi'. Believe me, we wanted to.

Slowly we lost communication with friends back home. Their faces became a blur. We heard of more lies concerning the former Mississippi pastor. A horrible scenario unraveled for their new pastor. We didn't want to know any more details. Some friends would call us with the latest news, but their calls did not help us. We eventually had to quit hearing from them.

Everywhere we turned, we were challenged. Stuck in a time warp between the world we had loved and the reality in front of us, we struggled to process it. We didn't blame God and we didn't blame ourselves. That would have made things easier but not better. All we knew was that we had to get a grip on life in this foreign world. We had to get over it so we could move beyond it. But we didn't know how. The grace of God was what held us together. It was a season of testing, and James 1:2-4, no matter what translation we read it in, didn't help us. We wanted God to fix it! He had other plans.

It came to me strongly one day that if I was going to get over it, I would have to walk out more than 20 years of what I had taught. I had to deal with the past and the present at the same time. I could no longer balance my hatred for what had happened to us with ministering to the needs of the youth staring me in the face each week. I had to become single focused on the opportunity in front of me.

Brokenness had to be dealt with from a base of faith and spiritual toughness. Forgiving the source of what had happened to me was a first step. I knew how to walk it out. The next step required more. The personal view of myself had to change from being a broken mess in a foreign land. I had to begin seeing myself as a vessel useful in the lives of the teenagers in front of me. They hadn't caused my brokenness. Neither had I. JoAn and I couldn't continue to live as victims of our circumstances. We needed to come back to life, not based on a change in our circumstances, but based on an inward reality of our life in Jesus Christ. We had to allow Him to be the author and finisher of our faith in our scattered times. We had to toughen up.

We also had to help our kids toughen up. The two older ones were facing life decisions in their career choices. The younger three were adapting to a new neighborhood, a new church, and a new educational environment. We had to toughen up spiritually if we were to help them. Equally important were the teenage faces staring at us each week at church.

TRANSFORMATION DURING THE BATTLE OF 1994

Our scattered times in Iowa were diverted back to God's bigger picture. We let go of the comparison game of judging Iowa and its people based on our 20 years of history in Mississippi. Mississippi had transitioned us, but Iowa would transform us. Iowa tested our sincerity and provided clarity for those transitions in our past. Ultimately, the years in Iowa transformed us. The small picture view of transitional times is at first deceptive. Transitional times require continual inward focus. Testing forces us to see beyond the immediate.

That handful of youth in Iowa would grow to more than a hundred in the five years we were there. We also would grow. Those years will forever be some of the best years of our life. But I had to own the moment that I was living rather than regret it. I had to get over Mississippi without ever leaving those precious people behind in my memories. I had to toughen up. Few transitions in our life have been as challenging as the Battle of 1994, but in every transition, there is testing. Here's the way I see it:

Transition + Testing = Transformation.

On multiple levels all three are happening in different areas of our life at the same time. Sometimes we get caught in the crossfire. Spiritual toughness grows relationally in those times through our faith in Jesus and His Word. But what about testing in good times? Good Times can also cause us to feel scattered. People who spend more time talking about what they're going through rather than what they're going to live scattered.

Settling into limiting mindsets and habits is subtle, like a house's foundation that slowly settles unnoticed. When we make a move of any kind that unsettles us, we find ourselves in scattered times that test us. The testing is real.

In what I've labeled 'The Battle of 1994', we did more than just make the choice to stop comparing Iowa to Mississippi. I had to stop going through the motions of my job and instead make conscious efforts to minister effectively. There's a huge difference between the two. Even if your job isn't ministry oriented, you have to recognize when you're just going through the motions in life. You have to keep your focus beyond the job at hand if you're going to grow yourself in the test.

Our unfamiliar became even more unfamiliar as the original lead pastor in Iowa changed and as my brother and his family relocated back to our home state of Florida. Suddenly, I had a blank slate. The major reasons we made the move were gone, and we were left going through the motions. When you're just going through the motions, they are typically someone else's motions. The routine of my daily job gravitated into what was expected. Routine may be wonderful for some, but for me routine is like being stuck in an elevator going nowhere with the mundane rotation of outdated elevator music. It numbs my mind. In the 'Battle of 1994', activating my greatest strengths was key to breaking the gravitational pull of being stuck in the traditional role of youth pastor.

Battles are best won in the areas of our strengths. When I began to lean into my strengths, I cracked the code and broke the gravitational pull of the traditional version of ministry. With a background in theatre and two decades of work in productions, I had learned that my mind requires creative stimuli. Like everyone else, my battles are best won in the areas of my strength. Our strengths are God-given instincts and talents that He created us to enjoy and explore. Moving in those areas frees us from the routine and predictable.

At the church, the physical space for the youth was huge. It could easily seat a hundred people at banquet tables. The ceiling sloped upward from eight feet to more than twenty. It had a small closet from which we served refreshments during Wednesday night youth services. The stage rose more than four feet high and created a psychological gulf disconnecting ministry from the people! Painted on the wall above the stage was an eagle that for some old timers was sacred.

I painted over the eagle. It was a great day. In fact, I repainted the entire room, tore down the beverage closet, built a large serviceable kitchen with running water and a refrigerator, and added a sound and light booth. I hung dozens of pictures of the current youth. And those are just the visuals. With a creative bias, my strengths went beyond just what people could see. We instituted a new attitude and perspective. Everything was about Jesus' being *passionately invested in growing youth into someone they could never be without His direction and intervention.*

In addition to my creative bias was my teacher bias and a growing leadership bias, as well. Combine these three biases, and everything I touched became targeted for a shake down.

When we break the gravitational pull of settling for anything less than who we really are, we will unsettle things and sometimes people. The fresh gravitational pull of our strengths may cause us to question the status quo of everything in our world. We may not be able to change that world. But we can definitely make changes in that world by activating our strengths. But first we have to change how we see ourselves in that world. We can do that best by believing in who we really are. Our new familiar must defy going backward to make congenial efforts with our past normal.

Remember in school that to prepare for the test, we had to know what was on the test. Our teacher knew. Your teacher may have taught from the test perspective. He or she probably made certain that whatever was on the test was also taught, and your classmates at large made it an issue if anything on the test had not been covered in class. Remember those days?

In real life, you make up the test. I'm not focused here on what your job description is; I'm focused on your strength description. The real test in life is to live out our strengths. If you are a person of faith, living out your strengths is directly tied to your faith. Both our faith and our strengths are keys to living forward in scattered times.

When I leaned fully into my strengths, everything changed in the 'Battle of 1994'! For example, when I taught youth how to deal with inferiority, I mixed the teaching with a little creativity. This mixture morphed into what became a yearly favorite that we called the 'Pity Prom'. It was a spoof on proms and allowed teenagers to dress as tacky and outlandish as they wanted. We played stupid games on purpose and ate yucky food. We mocked proms by crowning the king and queen of pity by an unfair voting method. Over a hundred youth from all over the area began attending the pity prom. It was born out of necessity with a bias toward all my strength areas. It flipped the stress associated with traditional proms to a fun night attacking inferiority. Everyone could equally engage in the Pity Prom. My bias for creativity won the day.

What happens when we begin to play the game of life with a bias for our strengths? We develop a new familiar! We begin to see opportunities in people and places that we previously viewed as limitations. The joy of life returns. We begin to be glad that we are who we are, regardless of where we are. Our confidence and effectiveness gain traction. We easily pass the test because we are living out our life with a bias that embraces our strengths.

But let's back up. When JoAnn and I began to let go of the critical and judgmental attitude that facilitated our comparison attack against Iowa, something else began to change. Our perspective changed and with it, our perception of ourselves in that perspective. We played our best strengths against the odds and changed the game we had been playing from 'Poor old me' to playing 'This is me and these are my strengths.' Doing so is always a win/win.

We intentionally began to be thankful for the sake of being thankful. We began to be grateful that God had not lost track of us. In fact, we began to notice the new 'breadcrumbs' of His presence. Life began to make sense.

As we chose to rejoice, we noticed that a small group of parents began to like us enough to engage with us on a more relational level. They became our top 20% of parental influencers. They influenced the other 80% of the parents and ran interference and provided clarity of vision. They became an unstoppable team for whom we are forever grateful.

As we rejoiced, we also began to see something similar among the youth. Some youth began to like hanging out with us. Consequently, we began to see them as the top 20% of influencers among the youth. Like the parents, these teenagers had influence on the other 80% of the youth. We poured ourselves into the top 20% of both groups. As the numbers grew, the influencers, both parents and youth, grew in leadership. Into whatever area I leaned, the influencers leaned with me. I count those five years among the best years of my life. But it all began as we changed ourselves and grew a bias for rejoicing rather than complaining. When you rejoice because you believe it is healthy to do so and unhealthy not to, something happens. Let me remind you again of why that works.

> *…when it seems as though you are facing nothing but difficulties, see it as an invaluable opportunity to experience the greatest joy that you can! For you know that when your faith is tested it stirs up power within you to endure all things. And then as your endurance grows even stronger it will release perfection into every*

part of your being until there is nothing missing and
nothing lacking.

JAMES 1:2-4

The King James version of this verse says: **'Count it all joy when you fall into divers temptations...'**. I remind you that the word 'count' comes from the base of a word meaning 'to govern.' Governing life in scattered times by rejoicing, even when we don't feel like it and life doesn't look like it should, means we rejoice anyway! The test in scattered and trying times is strategically decided by what governs our way through them. That means being grateful for who God is, regardless of what we see in our current circumstances.

Gratitude is not easy. In fact, gratitude requires God's grace more than our will power. Will power usually comes up short because it focuses on us. Will power is emotional. Governing our life based on gratitude for who God is keeps our focus on Him and His Word. But let's go deeper. Governing our life based on gratitude opens our eyes to fresh possibilities surfacing within us.

Governing our life in scattered times with gratitude for who God is must have a foundational truth to stand on. James' instructions give us that foundational truth. Truth is best grounded in what we know. Apparently, the scattered believers had lost something in the transition. That something was the essence of his letter. Remove this something, and the rest falls flat.

James states clearly: For you know that when your faith
is tested it stirs up power within you to endure all things.
And then as your endurance grows even stronger it will
release perfection into every part of your being until
there is nothing missing and nothing lacking.

JAMES 1:3-4

In my experience, nothing stirs up power like rejoicing in the Lord. Here's the secret sauce of life: Grace!

GRACE MAKES US RECEPTIVE TO FAITH

> *For it is by grace you have been saved through faith – and this is not from yourselves, it is the gift of God.*
> EPHESIANS 2:8 (KJV)

In unsettled and scattered times, lean into God's grace. Why? Because grace makes us receptive to faith. God's grace certainly preceded our commitment to the Lordship of Jesus Christ. Grace influences our heart to believe, thus making us receptive to faith. Where does this thought come from?

According to the Gospel of John, chapter 1 and verse 14, grace and truth came by Jesus Christ. It follows that wherever Jesus went, both of these life-giving forces went with Him. Imagine this: Whenever Jesus walked in a room, grace walked in with Him. Grace saturated the place. People He met were often people nothing like Him, and yet they fell in love with Him. The presence of His grace made them receptive to believing in whatever He was teaching. Faith rose up in the most unlikely people. Fishermen, tax collectors, prostitutes, religious leaders, and military men, to name a few, were drawn by faith into His Grace.

Those who granted Jesus an audience often did more than believe – they became grateful. They recognized who Jesus really was, and they became audibly grateful. Something else happened as well. Once grace abounded and they believed, gratitude became their new norm, and once gratitude took root, their generosity with others abounded. The news spread. The crowd followed. The world changed.

Here's what I've learned:

GRACE + GRATITUDE = GENEROSITY.

Passing whatever testing you're going through today requires the grace of God. Peter said in each of his letters (see verse 2 in I & II Peter) that he prayed for grace to be multiplied to believers! The quagmire of scattered times is best turned on its head when grace abounds. God emphatically told the Apostle Paul that grace was sufficient for whatever he was going through. Passing tests in scattered times requires the constant 'understudy' of grace. In whatever stage of life we're playing out, we need His grace standing by us in the wings.

It takes grace to be grateful in scattered times. Remember how James begins redirecting those persecuted and living in unfamiliar times: '**...when it seems as though you are facing nothing but difficulties, see it as an invaluable opportunity to experience the greatest joy that you can!**'

THE CHARACTER ISSUE

Something fresh clicked in our character during the Battle of 1994. The grace of God mixed with our gratitude for all that He is. Together they produced in us a fresh level of generosity. We began to invest more fully in the lives of those around us. Our investment in the parents as well as their children mirrored the bias of our strengths. Generosity should shine through our strengths. For us, we no longer lived focused on going backward to easier and more familiar times. As God proved Himself faithful in our present times, we grew fully engaged.

Don't miss the point in this section on testing. The point is that as we continually identify and move in the biased areas of our strengths something happens. The gravitational pull of our familiar past loses its grip. Our gift areas are released to others through the grace of God, not through the manipulation or force of our talents. It is through His grace that God gifts us in the tough moments we live.

The testing is never about us remaining steadfast in who we were in our last season. That mentality does not serve us or anyone else. We pass the test when we allow God to grow us into His image for our new season. It's His image clothed loosely in the framework of our strengths that opens others' eyes to who we really are. Suddenly, we see the world around us differently. Again, I remind you that testing is a character issue. Remember what Paul wrote to the Romans:

> *But that's not all! Even in times of trouble we have a joyful confidence, knowing that our pressures will develop in us patient endurance. And patient endurance will refine our character, and proven character leads us back to hope. And this hope is not a disappointing fantasy, because we can now experience the endless love of God cascading into our hearts through the Holy Spirit who lives in us!*
>
> ROMANS 5:3-5

In every season, regardless of the testing, the key is to lean into God's faithfulness. We do that best by continually leaning into His grace. God's grace fuels gratitude, and gratitude ushers in generosity.

7

THE LISTENING PRINCIPLE

*Listening is so close to loving that
most can't tell the difference.*
—*John Maxwell*

WHEN THE EARMUFFS COME OFF (ACTS 10 & 11)

Religious traditions had ear-muffled Peter from the greater audience for which Jesus died. The Gospel provided salvation for all people, not just the Jews, but Peter had not fully processed what we call the 'nearly too good to be true' Gospel. Peter, like some other early messengers, seemed tone deaf to the full revelation for whom God's new covenant was intended. That is, until the Holy Spirit pulled Peter's religious ear-muffs off on a rooftop in Joppa! The sound barrier of Peter's comfortable Jewish ministry was challenged mid-afternoon on that rooftop. Simon the Tanner's house is where it happened.

Peter was praying on the roof top while a meal was being prepared down below. Perhaps it was the smell of that meal's preparation that triggered hunger in Peter's mind. Regardless, the Holy Spirit took advantage of the moment to wreck Peter's world view of the Gospel's intent.

Out of nowhere, Peter, trance-like, saw a vision of sorts. A large sheet descending from the Heavens to earth appeared filled with all kinds of animals and reptiles and birds. A voice spoke to him: 'Rise, Peter; kill and eat!' 'Nothing doing,' thought Peter. Peter had never eaten anything considered unclean by the Jewish law. But the voice was persistent. 'What God has made clean, do not call common,' the voice continued. In fact, this voice repeated the same message three times. Odd, thought Peter.

Downstairs, there was more than a meal cooking. Men from Caesarea were knocking on the door. Unknown to Peter, they had come to retrieve him. Their master, Cornelius, had sent them to bring him to his house in Caesarea to share the Gospel. The problem was that like the unclean animals in Peter's vision, these men as well as their master's household were Gentiles!

Back on the rooftop, God continued expounding the vision to Peter. That's when in the Holy Spirit informed him of the three men waiting for him downstairs. Peter's instructions from the Holy Spirit were to go with the men and do so promptly! Once Peter came downstairs, his understanding of the vision connected with the messengers at the door. He made plans to depart for Caesarea.

The next morning, Peter and his team from Joppa, along with the men from Caesarea, set out. Entering the Gentiles' house, Peter found it jampacked with Cornelius' friends and relatives, all unclean Gentiles! Peter's opening words were apologetic. He made clear to all present how unlawful it was for a Jew to enter a Gentile's house. Pressing further, he explained that God had told him not to call anyone unclean or common. Peter, perhaps buying time, elaborated at length. His stop and go style of conversation must have hung awkwardly in the air.

Ultimately, God intervened. In the middle of Peter's rambling exposé on the life, death, and resurrection of Jesus, as well as on 'why' he and the gang had been preaching only to the Jews, the Holy Spirit showed up. In fact, He showed up as He had on the Day of Pentecost. Tongues and prophecy went vocal. Aghast! Peter wholeheartedly embraced that the Gospel was to be preached to everyone. Not given to slow moving actions, Peter commanded the whole house of gentile believers to be baptized in water! It was a great day for the Gospel of Jesus Christ.

Rumors of this unorthodox day in the life and ministry of Peter quickly reached Jerusalem. First, Peter was called on the carpet for being in a Gentile home. More disturbing to the status quo in Jerusalem were rumors that a whole bunch of gentiles at Cornelius' house received salvation, were filled with the Holy Spirit, and water baptized. Rumors of what happened rivalled the personal experience of the Church founders at Pentecost. It was a pivoting, head scratching moment for the Church at large.

Peter defended himself as best he could, but the cat was out of the bag. It was open season for Gentiles hearing the Gospel. 'Who was I to stand in God's way?' Peter concluded in what we would call today a *drop the mic* moment! The earmuffs came off. Jewish leaders came on board. Game changer times followed. The gospel opened to the 'whosoever will believe' crowd as God had intended.

But before the game changer could happen, the earmuffs had to come off Peter's ears. The Holy Spirit's strategic move on the rooftop back in Joppa began the game changer. Peter's preconceived mindset had to be challenged. He had to really listen to what the Holy Spirit was saying, even when it went crossways with his original assumptions. Perhaps he had previously missed a few points. Processing what happened on the roof top in Joppa with what happened at Cornelius' house changed the trajectory of the Gospel. Both experiences changed Peter's mindset. You can read all about it in Acts 10 and 11. But the point in these next two chapters is twofold: listening and wisdom! This story points in that direction. Growing in our faith is filled with challenges to our preconceived ideas. Listening is not only key, but listening is strategic. The wisdom of God needs an open ear!

PROMPT LISTENING!

Listening repositions us and puts truth within our grasp.

Reaching back into James' letter to those scattered by persecution, he makes it clear that listening is a priority.

> *...Be quick to listen, but slow to speak. And be slow to become angry, for human anger is never a legitimate tool to promote God's righteous purpose.*
> JAMES 1:19-20

The purpose of those scattered by persecution was to 'promote God's purpose!' But when anyone is in the shuffling chaos of scattered times, being quick to speak tends to overrule the luxury of taking time to listen. James made efforts in his letter to help them prioritize listening. His point was not just about them listening to each other. His main point was that they needed to tune in to the Holy Spirit. When listening to the Holy Spirit gets muffled, our back and forth with others becomes a mixture of sounds and voices. We get sidetracked.

What does it mean to be quick to listen? By using the word 'quick,' James meant *prompt!* Think of it in the way we have to be promp in listening to the GPS. Otherwise…well you get the point. Similarly, listening to the Holy Spirit is intended to reposition us. Remember that for the Gentiles to hear the Gospel, the messengers of that Gospel had to be turned in a certain direction. Listening, followed by corresponding action, initiates movement. Faith in what we hear moves us resolutely in a certain direction. We have to pull truth into our conscience awareness and act on it. As believers, we are expected to experience relevant downloads of God's wisdom. Promptness to hear is where it all begins.

When Jesus finished telling a parable, He and his disciples would engage in a little one on twelve time. Before explaining a parable, Jesus often explained the key to understanding it. Listening was that key! Here's what Jesus said in the Gospel of Mark:

> *Be diligent to understand the meaning behind everything you hear, for as you do, more understanding will be given to you. And according to the depth of your longing to understand, much more will be added to you. For those who listen with open hearts will receive more revelation.* **But those who don't listen with open hearts will lose what little they think they have!**
>
> MARK 4:24-25

Got it? Our thinking lacks continuity. Thoughts racing through our minds intermingle. Responsibilities run on one train of thought while our search for spiritual perspective runs on another. In the haste of the moment, we tend to run both trains of thought at the same time. The result? A little of this and a little of that! Promptness and an open heart are keys to effective listening.

Jesus' point brings clarity to why *we see but don't perceive* and why *we hear but don't understand*. Read again what Jesus said: *'according to the depth of your longing to understand, much more will be added to you. For those who listen with open hearts will receive more revelation.'* Two things are required:

1. Longing to understand.
2. Open hearts.

Surfing on top of whatever the Lord is communicating to us or what someone else is communicating isn't enough. Surfing on top lacks revelation. In theatre terms, the line spoken without understanding of why a character speaks it leaves the audience in the dark. Consequently, the audience is robbed of the subtext behind the spoken text! Clarity begins with a promptness to listen, but it doesn't end there. That's why Jesus pulled his disciples aside to deepen their understanding.

Our promptness to listen and respond to the direction and intervention of God is the game changer that James was reaching for in his letter. The story of Peter in Acts illustrates the value of promptly responding to what we hear. Obviously, both Peter and Cornelius listened and promptly responded to what they heard. Their swiftness to hear was followed by immediate action, just as the Holy Spirit expected. Between their swiftness to hear and their quickness to act, it was their willingness to meditate and process what they heard that brought them revelation of God's intentions. Our willingness to meditate and process what we're hearing is vital.

Nothing as dramatic as a descending sheet full of unclean animals has ever happened to me. But here's the point. Listening is made difficult when we have preconceived ideas that are out of sync with their purpose. The same is true when we live ignorant of how God thinks. Putting what we hear in the context of the speaker's point of view is required. Understanding fully requires extended time to process what has been said. This same practice and processing on a spiritual level alerts us to God's intended direction and intervention. Wisdom results.

THE WISDOM CONNECTION

In the opening lines of his letter, James tells us that whenever we lack wisdom in trying times that we are to ask for it. The revelation we need is always in the wisdom the Holy Spirit freely gives. But more than just hearing words of wisdom is developing a relationship with the Holy Spirit.

Jesus teaches us about the Holy Spirit in the Gospel of John 14-16. The Holy Spirit is the presence of God on the earth today. In the lives of all believers, He desires to teach, guide, comfort, and father us. His presence in our lives requires our promptness and hunger to perceive rather than to just see, to understand rather than to just hear. We have to recognize the difference.

Half of learning to listen is deciding to listen. Our relationship with the Holy Spirit comes down to learning:
- How God sees us.
- How God thinks about us.
- How God cares for us.

Understanding these three things tenders a more accurate spiritual trajectory. God's reference point matters. Listening from His point is a game changer. Take your time here. These seven points can change how you hear when you are listening. Allow the Holy Spirit to teach, guide and father you through these points of view. Don't rush it. Don't be anxious. Focus.

LISTENING FROM GOD'S POINT OF VIEW

1. Listen to God as someone made in His image.

So God created man in his own image, in the image of God he created him; male and female he created them. And God blessed them. And God said to them, 'Be fruitful and multiply and fill the earth and subdue it, and have dominion over the fish of the seas, and over the birds of the heavens and over every living thing that moves on the earth'.

GENESIS 1:27-28 (ESV)

In Christ you have the capacity to see yourself differently. The redeemed version of yourself isn't hinged to your past! You're a new creation.

2. Listen to God as a dearly loved child of God.

Be imitators of God in everything you do, for then you will represent your Father as his beloved sons and daughters. And continue to walk surrendered to the extravagant love of Christ, for he surrendered his life as a sacrifice for us. His great love for us was pleasing to God, like an aroma of adoration – a sweet healing fragrance.

EPHESIANS 5:1-2

Walk and listen as one surrendered to the extravagant love of Christ. Listen from His viewpoint of you as a dearly loved child. You are His favorite. Never doubt His love for you nor His desire to listen to you.

3. **Listen to the God who perceives your every move, thought, word and step.**

Lord, you know everything there is to know about me. You perceive every movement of my heart and soul, and you understand my every thought before it even enters my mind. You are so intimately aware of me, Lord. You read my heart like an open book and you know all the words I'm about to speak before I even start a sentence! You know every step I will take before my journey even begins. You've gone into my future to prepare the way, and in kindness you follow behind me to spare me from the harm of my past.

PSALM 139:1-5

Live with the awareness that God goes before us and He comes after us. He is always present, always engaging, and always directing. Listen for Him in the context of these verses. We are not robots. We still have a will. We make choices. How does God know our every move? He knows our heart. As we renew our mind, our heart changes.

4. **Listen from the point of view that you have been made mysteriously complex.**

I thank you, God, for making me so mysteriously complex!

PSALM 139:14

There is more to us than what we see physically. We're part of something bigger than just ourselves. Our uniqueness is complex when compared to our natural understanding. Scientist who study the human body know how complex we are physically. But we are more than our physical make up. God made us complex in the way we think, emote, and how we are attracted to the people and places where we add the most value. Our complexity makes us uniquely valuable for the times we're living. He made us in His image. He fabricated us into the multidimensional version of Himself as it pleased Him.

5. Understand that God created you to be you before you became you!

> *You saw who you created me to be before I became me!*
> PSALM 139:16

God is ever present and always has been. The depth of this statement should stop us in our tracks. The impact of it should prompt intentional listening. No one is an accident. God planned you. Artistically, physically, mentally, and emotionally, He created you. He placed you in the time frame of His choice. The world is less when you're not fully you.

6. Listen from the perspective that your fulfillment comes from God's fullness:

> *And now out of his fullness we are fulfilled! And from him we receive grace heaped upon more grace! Moses gave us the Law, but Jesus the Anointed One, unveils truth wrapped in tender mercy. No one has ever gazed upon the fullness of God's splendor except the uniquely beloved Son, who is cherished by the Father and held close to his heart. Now he has unfolded to us the full explanation of who God truly is!*
> JOHN 1:16-18

The rush hour traffic version of our faith misses this point. Our fulfillment in life comes from Him. He is the one who *'unveils truth wrapped in tender mercy.'* Course corrections of God's kind come wrapped in mercy, not condemnation! The Holy Spirit unfolds explanations of who God is in terms we can understand. Listening is our part. The rest is His part. He unfolds His grace and truth. In His fullness we are fulfilled. The more connected we are to His word, the greater our fulfillments.

7. **Listen from the perspective that your cup is suppose to overflow!**

> *The Lord is my best friend and my shepherd. I always have more than enough. He offers a resting place for me in his luxurious love. His tracks take me to an oasis of peace, the quiet brook of bliss. That's where he restores and revives my life. He opens before me pathways to God's pleasure and leads me along in his footsteps of righteousness so that I can bring honor to his name. Lord, even when your path takes me through the valley of deepest darkness, fear will never conquer me, for you already have! You remain close to me and lead me through it all the way. Your authority is my strength and my peace. The comfort of your love takes away my fear. I'll never be lonely, for you are near. You become my delicious feast even when my enemies dare to fight. You anoint me with the fragrance of your Holy Spirit, you give me all I can drink of you until my heart overflows. So why would I fear the future? For your goodness and love pursue me all the days of my life. Then afterward, when my life is through, I'll return to your glorious presence to be forever with you!*
>
> PSALM 23

Reading scripture as if you've never heard it before brings fresh eyes to the mix. Varying the translations we read, should reinforce and challenge the application of what we've previously known. Psalm 23 is like the 'circle of life' in a spiritual concept. From start to finish, the psalmist finds God close and more than enough. The inventory of our lives is not limited to what we can physically calculate. Our heart is preset to overflow with His presence. This overflow is not restricted to a once in a lifetime moment. His presence just is! Life is meant to be full.

HOW TO PROCESS GOD'S POINT OF VIEW:

Reflect quietly on these truths on a regular basis. Give them time to sink in. Be absorbed by them. Process them into all the broken places of your life. Set some additional time aside just to listen to them. Really listen. Listen from a baseline of truth that makes you more receptive to hearing what else is on God's heart. Listen completely without judging yourself or discounting yourself from who He says you are.

The Apostle Peter drives home these seven points in his first letter to the church.

> *But you are God's chosen treasure – priests who are kings, a spiritual "nation" set apart as God's devoted ones. He called you out of darkness to experience his marvelous light, and now he claims you as his very own. He did this so that you would broadcast his glorious wonders throughout the world. For at one time you were not God's people, but now you are. At one time you knew nothing of God's mercy, because you hadn't received it yet, but now you are drenched with it.*
> I PETER 2:9-10

God is always speaking, but don't expect an audible voice. Expect His will and thoughts to grow and unfold for you. I find that the Holy Spirit impresses on me a scripture or idea. It takes my mind longer than it should to make that scripture or idea priority for exploration. But once I become intentionally focused, it begins to unfold. It begins to open with the level of clarity I need or will need in the future. God works ahead of us!

LISTENING REPOSITIONS US

Think back through Gideon's story (Judges 6-7) in Chapter One. I find traces of change happening before the angel shows up in the winepress. When Gideon begins questioning where the God of the miraculous is, his curiosity increases. His perspective slowly loses its edge. When Gideon listened to the angel, his mindset began to shift.

Consider Moses, the murderer, on the backside of the desert. Was the sight of the burning bush the first to draw him away? Not that there were other burning bushes, but I believe Moses was schooled to watch for unusual sights. His curiosity had been nurtured previously. God moved on his preferences for the unusual. He does the same for us. He knows what attracts our curiosity and what draws our listening ear.

God plays with what gets our attention. He really knows us. He knows what makes us tick. His approach to Gideon is different than his approach to David, Samson, or Joseph. Our sensitivity to God is tweaked by the Holy Spirit. Because we are made in the image of God, we can connect with Him. We can play on the way God made us just as He does in reaching us!

Our relationship with God through the Holy Spirit is not meant to be competitive. Paul warns us not to compare ourselves among ourselves (II Corinthians 10:12). God is as unique as we are unique, and we are as unique as He is. He connects with our uniqueness.

Our strengths are in our uniqueness. He draws from our strengths. The Holy Spirit plays on the way we were made.

When God draws us out of darkness, He draws us to Himself. He longs for intimacy with us. He dotes on us. He loves us the way He made us. We, too, must come to that point. He repositions us by His Word. He hints at our strengths until we embrace them. He hints at purposes until we own them. He hints at His directions and interventions until we allow them. Listening is always key.

As we respond to Jesus, the Holy Spirit fathers us the rest of the way. We become the transformational version of God's intended vision of us. When our hunger for Him reaches an intoxicating hunger, transformation goes into overdrive. It matters that we learn to listen and live curious of His ways.

Listening triggers faith. Faith exponentially makes us sensitive to the heart cry of God. We become sensitive to His heart's conversation and Kingdom agendas. The Holy Spirit invades our conversations. We begin to interject his thoughts, teaching, leading, and fathering in random conversations. He uses us to drop *breadcrumbs* to generate awareness in others that He is working in them.

God works in us so that we begin to broadcast His glorious wonders into a dark world! In line with this understanding, we realize that our momentary difficulties are nothing compared to the 'invaluable opportunities' afforded us. We awaken to the significance that our strengths are intended to impact this world.

Scattered times become times of great rejoicing when we believe that the trying of our faith changes us. We listen more intently because we know power is in the wisdom that follows. We speak and take action. Our lives take on the significance God intended when He created us!

THE ANATOMY OF LISTENING

Allow me to share a few principles that may help others in the room. They, too, are scattered by the times. God is playing on the way He made them. We are intended to be a major player in some of their lives.

On a practical or academic level, there are four stages of listening. Whenever I train leaders, these four stages lay the groundwork for the discussion and exercises that follow. These four stages played out in the opening text of Peter's rooftop experience.

STAGE ONE: PERCEPTION

First, we have to perceive that something worth our attention requires our attention. That means we have to tune in to it. That's also where we usually miss it. Peter tuned in, but he was a little slow perceiving the direction God was taking him. That's also where we miss it. Perceiving and tuning in fosters an exchange where two parties connect. Connecting is where relationships thrive. Our relationship with God is no different.

STAGE TWO: INTERPRETATION

Secondly, we have to get clarity on what is really meant by what we're hearing. Peter's understanding evolved. The Holy Spirit's message to Peter was a major game changer. It altered his preconceived *everything*. Extending grace to the Gentiles was a radical departure from what had become the norm. The key for us is that we have to be sure we understand the message in the context it's given before we judge the message. Our opinions about the messenger can taint our understanding of the message. Sometimes it's helpful to separate the two. Other times, as with the Holy Spirit, it's helpful to combine the two!

STAGE THREE: EVALUATION

Thirdly, evaluation is premature until we have accurate understanding. Clarity of the message gives us the platform needed to evaluate it. We need to put it in the right context. Peter's vision on the rooftop made sense in the context of what was happening at the front door. More than just listening was required of Peter. He had to connect the conversation on the roof with the conversation at the front door. His evaluation of the two conversations motivated his prompt action.

STAGE FOUR: ACTION

Finally, action follows evaluation. Action in Acts 10 was a 'pack it up and let's go somewhere way outside our comfort zone' type of action. But that level of immediate action is not always required. Even Peter waited until the next morning. Once at Cornelius' house, he was still processing the whole 'Grace and Gentile' thing when the Holy Spirit jumped in and made a move. God moves quickly whenever there is a fresh hunger in the room for more of Himself. As you share Jesus, don't be surprised when God has already prompted your audience to receive what you've come to share. God goes before us. He prepares the way.

The Gentiles' hunger plus God's message to Cornelius prompted quick action. Cornelius sent messengers to Peter immediately. Peter moved promptly. His fresh revelation of Jesus' 'Go into all the world and make disciples' command prompted his action.

LISTENING IN CHANGING TIMES

> **Listening is so close to loving, most people can't tell the difference.**
>
> JOHN MAXWELL

Questioning the relevance of old mindsets is rarely on our daily shopping list. But questioning is an exercise that can keep us relevant. We have to decide to be flexible enough to reassemble what we hear in the immediate without the limitations of our yesterdays. If Peter had not been willing to unthink his preconceived Jewish mindset, he would never have entertained sharing the gospel with Gentiles. Nothing changed in what Peter understood to be the power of the gospel. What changed was his limited view of his audience. This is the type of unthinking we need to invest ourselves in. It's a stretch. It's part of the ongoing prompting of the Holy Spirit's direction and intervention, not just for us, but for the benefit of others. Our audience is always changing.

Remember those matching tests in school? Remember finishing the test and being ready to turn it in, when suddenly you began to unthink an answer? You suddenly realized something didn't make sense. You feared the whole house of cards was about to collapse. Perhaps your answers had been recorded out of sequence on the answer sheet. You realized everything was out of line. Good thing you did some unthinking.

LISTENING TO GOD

Tuning in also requires tuning out! We're never fully listening until we tune out the unnecessary. Let's go back to Proverbs 3:5-6

> **In all your ways acknowledge him and he will direct your path.**
>
> (KJV)

I know you've heard this before in this book, but I doubt it hit you like it may now. Why? Because now the very same scripture comes in a totally different context. That was my intention. What if you acknowledge what you're hearing from Him? James knew that in scattered times we're more prone to speak and get angry than we are to listen. Listening in order to better acknowledge what God is conveying clears our God-given path. We finally think it. We speak it. We follow it.

FAITH COMES BY LISTENING

Remember when people said to you: 'You've got lots of potential'? What they didn't say was that potential is just that – potential! Alone, potential never changes the world. World changers learn to develop their potential. Experience is not the best teacher. When experience alone becomes our teacher, we live void of reflective thinking. Experience alone doesn't go deep enough. If we are to own the truth God is revealing to us, we have to reflect on it. Talking about potential doesn't develop it. Potential, like truth, has to be acted on, not just noticed!

Truth at a *revelationary* level still has to be acted upon. God's truth is relationally focused. Faith and truth are a liberating combo. They thrive in a relationship with the Holy Spirit. Regardless of what we're going through, the Holy Spirit wants to connect with us.

> *Faith comes by listening and listening by the Word of God.*
> ROMANS 10:17 (KJV)

If faith really comes by listening, we need to take inventory of who or what we're listening to. How? Listen to what you constantly talk about. That will reveal what you really believe as well as its source. Jesus said that '*out of the abundance in our heart* (thoughts and words), *our mouth speaks.*' Since we believe more of what we hear ourselves say than what we hear others say, hearing our own words has life-changing relevance. Faith brings to life whatever we are predominately listening to. Why? Because that is the principle by which faith operates. Faith comes by what consistently we hear.

However, talking our faith becomes a flawed effort if we make it a legalistic endeavor. For example, guarding our words to give the appearance that we're walking in faith is deceptive. We're the first one it deceives. That's why James says that being a hearer of the Word but not a doer of the Word is deceptive. Doing begins in a believing heart, but it doesn't stop there.

Just because we police our spoken vocabulary doesn't guarantee that our corresponding actions are of faith. Listening to our heart, not just our words, discerns between truth in action and truth that is just noise. Course corrections based on truth turn our lives resolutely in transitional directions. Transformation follows.

Listening keeps us focused on adjusting what we naturally see in the mirror to what we see spiritually in God's Word. God's Word is intended to lift us into a realm of grace beyond our scattered moments and crisis. There is more than one reason that faith pleases God. Faith keeps us in an on-going conversation with the Holy Spirit. His fathering of us is critical at all times.

The Holy Spirit fathers us beyond the banter of our familiar and ushers us to the threshold of His wisdom. Wisdom gives us the critical edge needed to navigate through the transitional times between what was once familiar and what will soon become our new familiar. Wisdom is part of the bridge to our new familiar. That's the theme of the next chapter.

8

THE WISDOM
PRINCIPLE

> *I begin with humility, I act with humility, I*
> *end with humility. Humility leads to clarity.*
> —*Eric Greitens*

Wisdom transforms information into revelation. Sometimes the missing link in our most trying times is just a matter of connecting the dots between what we know and what wisdom can reveal. Wisdom comes in chunks of revelation that connect our dots of information into a fresh perspective of the way things really are or can become.

WISDOM IS THE 'SUBTEXT' OF REVELATION

As a theatre person, I can compare wisdom to the unspoken subtext hiding beneath the written dialogue in a script. In undergraduate classes, I learned that only knowing the lines or spoken text in a scene painted an incomplete picture of the playwriters' intent. The director and actor have to find the appropriate 'subtext' or the motivation behind the dialogue's words. From the subtext, the actor also develops an 'inner monologue' of the character's thoughts. Those are thoughts the character is thinking before and during their words and actions. How? By searching for the 'why' that best justifies the character's spoken words and action. Once the subtext becomes clear, the actor develops the corresponding emphasis. Wisdom provides the subtext and clarity that the Holy Spirit brings into our lives. He gives us the appropriate inner monologue to think.

Leveraging Godly wisdom brings wisdom into play regardless of how scattered life becomes. Wisdom provides a fresh perspective beyond the emotional turmoil we may be experiencing. Meditating on scripture followed by reflective thinking resets our perspective of God's intentions. Like the playwright who authors a script, God is both the author and finisher of our faith.

When wisdom gives us revelation, it's like putting on 3D glasses to see the full depth of a movie as the director intends. With Godly wisdom, the end game of our scattered times gains traction. The pieces come together. We begin to move forward. We grow from a stumbling version of ourselves into living the organic, healthy version. The measured wisdom of the Holy Spirit aligns within the true purposes for which God created us.

Wisdom is hindered when our relationship with God is more of a spectator sport than the ongoing relationship we were designed to follow. How does this work? Everything with God works by faith. In Jesus is our God-given wisdom. We pursue His wisdom by faith. Our relationship with Him through the Holy Spirit should be an ongoing conversation. When His perspective becomes our perspective, we enjoy an open door back-and-forth dialogue with Him through the Holy Spirit. Godly wisdom should be trending more than anything else in our daily walk. Allowing unfamiliar circumstances to blur our dialogue with the Holy Spirit also blurs God's intention and wisdom. That's when we experience a blindfolded clarity.

Scattered times intensify when we demand that God speak to us the same way He did yesterday. As parents, we don't speak to our grown children in the same way we did when they were toddlers. Imagine the disciples mandating that Jesus teach them every day on a hillside with 5,000 men plus women and children! We can't program God like we do our computers. He wants relationship. What we really want are the repeated feelings of His presence in the same portions and versions of yesterday's emotions! This is not realistic or what we need. We need Him.

What happens in our relationship with friends when they start to change how they talk about things? We begin to see our relationship with them as a blurry mixture of what used to be familiar with what's trending in their present life. They need us to get on the current page with them. Memories are memories, but relationships have to grow. Life-long friendships integrate different conversations and experiences as we mature and grow. That's why we count on them. The same is true in our relationship with God. He is always in the authoring and finishing mode, which expects our relationship with Him to keep growing. Our relationship with Him shouldn't be threatened by what we consider unwelcome changes that we didn't originate or expect. Listen up. Don't miss this next point.

**God knows where we need to focus today
to meet tomorrow's challenges.**

What happens when we dig in our heels and want our relationship with God to stay on the same conversational or emotional level from which it began? We grieve what He wants to reveal to us, but revelation reveals something we haven't realized or activated before. That's wisdom in action. God has wisdom to give us what we need in scattered times and beyond. Don't limit Him.

Remember the confusion in Nicodemus' first conversation (John 3:1-21) with Jesus? Nicodemus wanted the facts. He wanted Jesus to reveal his connection to Father God! Instead, Jesus gave him revelation. Isn't Nicodemus like us? We want the facts. We want our dots connected. Instead, the Holy Spirit gives us revelation and expects us to think about it. God speaks wisdom. We hear a disconnect. Our emotions triage such moments as living in a no man's land. We find His unfamiliar tactics threatening. The transition God authors in us isn't always comfortable. We turn a deaf ear and become lonely, confused and stressed. We blame God.

When we interpret the turn of events in a new season as one that is unjust, we become even more scattered. Chaos results. It's God's fault—we didn't see it coming. It's like He turned the page and initiated a new chapter in our life, but He didn't warn us! We have no road map by which to navigate, but maybe, just maybe, in the rhythm of God's authoring and finishing, we missed a beat! That beat is the rhythm of wisdom.

Unless we leverage Godly wisdom into the mix of what He is authoring and finishing in our life, guess what—our life becomes a daily improvisation. We adlib our way unnecessarily through scattered times. Those scattered by persecution 2,000 years ago were no better at improvisation without Godly wisdom than we are. We need wisdom to make a grand entrance and initiate the plot changes needed. But we have to live tuned in as diligent listeners in every season of life.

Wisdom helps us realize that in every season, some of our familiar will make an exit and never reenter! Unfamiliar cast members make entrances. Their time on stage leverages the momentum

God intended so that our story can regain traction. The new set changes are for the next act of life. Wisdom helps us realize that some of the thoughts with which we've been clothing our mind aren't current or appropriate for our new season.

Wisdom helps us embrace the fact that our new chapter comes with blank pages. We need God's wisdom to fill in those blanks. Don't fill them with murmuring and complaining. Work out your salvation. (Philippians 2:12-15 (NIV)). Prioritize time with wisdom. Revelation always stands ready and waiting to make its grand entrance! Asking for wisdom is the cue God is waiting for.

JAMES' PAST

Let's pull back the curtain on James' past. Running parallel with the wisdom we need today are the issues from which James ripped the band aid from 2,000 years ago. He knew that life gets scattered when we're not paying attention. We know that most of the time we aren't. Here's a little background on the writer of this 'in your face wakeup call' to the first century church—and to us!

James was a half-brother of Jesus. Most scholars believe that James didn't see his older brother as the Messiah until after his death and resurrection. Let's go with that thought. What was the unbelieving brother of the Christ thinking during those three years of his brother's ministry? Wrap your brain around this possibility:

He viewed Jesus' life from outside the inner circle of the twelve disciples that traveled with Christ. He also had to process the controversies that surrounded Jesus. The whip thing in the temple probably messed with James' mind. So did his brother's most controversial teachings about who He kept inferring that He was. If

James didn't believe that whole 'messiah' discourse, what did he believe? No one knows.

Adding to the above controversy was his mother's inner circle of Marys! There is a cluster of people named Mary throughout the Gospels. They were probably in and out of James' house. His unbelief didn't dampen their faith. They lived and huddled daily in full excitement mode. And James?

James probably felt scattered. He felt confused. Worse, his disbelief separated him from his mother's excitement. He may have distanced himself to keep the peace. With whom could he talk? Where could he go? What sounding board would tolerate his transparency? Who would tolerate him venting his moods? See, life was as real and complicated 2,000 years ago as it is today. Our religious mindset has to get over it! To get the full impact of this letter to scattered people, we have to keep peeling the onion on James' pre-Christian moments.

In light of his pre-faith life, James' letter is written with keen insight into the issues with which he and most scattered believers wrestle. Thus, the poignant difference between our traditional read and a fresh understanding comes shouting at us from every page. James' understanding of scattered times mixed with the wisdom the Holy Spirit packs fresh revelation and knowledge. Let's just call it wisdom.

James highlights the issues scattered people deal with because he had brushed against those same issues up-close and personal. His letter is more authentic and confrontational than a first read may give. Once we get lost in the famous verses, we lose the relevancy he intended. His language and word choices deliver an edgy, fathering element. James may push a few of your buttons. It pushes a few of mine. Why? It demands adjustments.

'**Scattered as seeds sown**' opens the passage. Obviously, the early believers' emotions and their processing of the times had loosened their grasp on the spiritual truths they should have held close. Unexpected geographic changes had taken them out of their comfort zone. Uprooted and planted into an unfamiliar world with heavy Gentile influence, they found themselves profoundly emotional. The drive-by of their conflicting perspectives challenged them mentally and spiritually. They were a transitional mess.

In scattered times, it's difficult to sort out what's driving our 'inner monologue.' Remember 'inner monologue' refers to the thoughts that bring the actor to speak the words the audience hears. It takes a different brand of toughness to monitor our personal 'inner monologue' when times get scattered. We either play the gate keeper of our inner conversations or fill in the blanks with our own unabridged monologue.

Let's be fair with the recipients of James' letter. Their faith was new, their environment was new, their challenges were new, and their processing of information was hit and miss. By hit and miss, I mean undeveloped. They lacked wisdom. The gravitational pull of both their past and present was wreaking havoc. Their life teetered between two familiars, the former one and the future one. They were scattered in between both.

Inexperienced or scattered times don't give us a pass on Proverbs 23:7. The principle stands true regardless of our level of readiness. King James says: *As a man thinketh in his heart, so is he*. Yes, those sown like seeds probably knew the battlefield was in their mind. They knew that they were ultimately responsible for being the gatekeeper of their thought life. But knowledge without personal revelation and commitment in the moment we are living doesn't give us the traction needed to fully engage.

With that in mind, James' choice of words are spot on. Here's how I see the reality that James was confronting. I doubt he knew he was writing a letter that later generations would bind in the book we call the Bible, but God knew. His understanding of their times is based on knowledge and revelation from his own pre-Jesus experience. He writes based on the Holy Spirit's desire to provide revelation that will father believers. James, like most first century apostles, lived in a world of revelation.

The apostles wrestled with three historic dimensions of Israel's history: the past, the present, and their understanding of the future. We wrestle with the same. James' life had never been black and white. His life had always been complicated, but he offers his readers little slack for dealing with their scattered life. In fact, he doesn't let them off the hook. He holds them accountable. He plows headfirst and lets the chips fall where they may.

James knew that if they asked for wisdom in their wavering and doubting state of mind, their faith would not retrieve what was needed. Their image of themselves probably reminded him of the grasshopper images of the Israelites standing on the edge of the Promised Land. Remember, the Israelites mentally froze. Perhaps he figured his readers literally saw themselves as 'seeds scattered for destruction' instead of as 'seeds sown for the harvest.'

James saw them as actively doing a lot of double-talking and double-listening. Their focus was so divided that James suspected that they were blaming everything on God. They were so vocal in their anger that attempts of the Holy Spirit to redirect their thinking had fallen on deaf ears. James pulled this thread throughout his letter. His scattered readers were the opposite of being quick to listen. Quick to listen had been drowned long ago by their tendency to angrily rush to speak. How did James know that? He may have been remembering his own years of unbelief. He pushed forward.

The Word would have given them the wisdom they needed, but as we know, when wisdom becomes mixed with anxiety and anger, it becomes polluted. Their speech, like their inner monologue, had become cruel and sarcastic. With one another, they were harsh, abrupt, and judgmental. In their loneliness, they showed partiality and prejudice. They lived out of sync with the Lord's mercy. Judgement came easy. Condemnation thrived. Their needs had gone unmet. They grew more and more dishonorable and without love for one another. Consequently, they lived judgmental without mercy. Their faith, compromised by their vocal rhetoric, was without works, without fruit and certainly without the life-giving force they desperately needed.

At best, they had become raving teachers of what they were not living. Words left their lips like unbridled horses running wild, and James tagged them as such. Poison spewed from their mouths with blessing and cursing, jealousy and selfishness. They thought themselves wise but behind closed doors when the lights went out, they found themselves empty and ignorant, broken and forsaken. James remembered the feeling. His fathering instincts would win the day for them. But not yet!

> *Where jealousy and selfishness are uncovered, you will*
> *also find many troubles and every kind of meanness.*
> JAMES 3:16

They had given themselves to insider quarreling and fighting. Their anger had squelched asking God for anything. Somewhere deep inside they knew that asking with selfish motives would reap more of God's silence, but they did it anyway. In the spiral of their downward thinking, they had become friends with the world. Their compromise had made them enemies of God! No one wanted to admit that. No one ever does.

The Good News: God remained jealous for them. He remained wanting them. At this point the letter pivots. James begins to help them reposition their thinking. As he strategically writes, **'God gives grace to the humble.'** He begins washing them with the principle of drawing near to God so He will draw near to them. He encourages them to clean their hands; referring to their compromising works. He encourages them to purify their hearts from doublemindedness. He addresses their need for simplicity. He asserts that humbling themselves before God will result in God lifting them. The chink in their hardened hearts begins to heal. God's grace rushes in, even cascades, strengthening them in all their broken places.

He encourages them not to speak against each other. Less they over commit to turning their thinking around on a dime, he gives them practical advice. 'Don't tell God what you're going to do tomorrow,' he coaches. Tomorrow isn't promised. Do the right thing, don't stand around just talking about it. 'Establish your heart,' he says. 'Be steadfast,' he challenges. 'Wait patiently as farmers do for their harvest,' he concludes. Then James goes pastoral. Pray for one another. Confess your sins. Be healed. Start today!

Finally, James writes the famous verse that we often quote. There is a tenderness in this part. You can almost hear him slowing down. Methodically, he seems to weave them into a new version of themselves.

> *Confess and acknowledge how you have offended one another and then pray for one another to be instantly healed, for tremendous power is released through the passionate, heartfelt prayer of a godly believer.*
> JAMES 5:16

Wisdom is found in the letter's entirety. Wisdom is the 'principle thing' where both the Book of Proverbs and the Letter of James come full circle. Implementing wisdom is different than just knowing it. But just knowing it was their starting point. James provided more.

> *'Wisdom is proven by all her children!'*
>
> LUKE 7:35 (NIV)

How do we become children of wisdom? Can we regain the wisdom we need in scattered times? How do we become students of God's wisdom? Does it take more than one read? How do we move from moments that scatter us into moments that stabilize us? Glad you asked.

Who knows how many times they read and reread his letter? Or how many times they sobbed? What Satan had meant for destruction, James knew the grace of God would redeem. He also knew they would change the world, and they really did. From their scattered lives, wisdom shifted them forward. They became the pioneers of the faith, as God intended. Good for them. Great for us.

We also know that James' wisdom and truth wrapped in bluntness still offers a way through the scattered times of our contemporary life. Look around you and you will find previously scattered people walking in the grace of recovery.

Let me ask you a few questions. What chapter in your journey does grace need to rewrite? Will you allow it? Do you really believe that God's grace, like God's wisdom, is a page turner? Do you want to turn the page in your life's story?

Before we go deeper, lets reflect on the absolutes from James' letter but in 'proverb' form. Hope you find these truths worth leveraging into your daily walk.

JAMES' PROVERBS AND WISDOM

In everything, you can see invaluable opportunities.

The trying of faith stirs up power within us to develops endurance.

Endurance builds character.

God is more ready to give us wisdom than we are to ask Him for it.

Seek wisdom without doubting, and we will receive.

Keeping faith strong in difficult times brings untold blessings.

God is incapable of tempting anyone with evil; it's not in His DNA.

Evil desires give birth to evil actions.

God's truth leverages life-giving truth. His truth, like His word, is infallible.

Listen quickly, speak slowly, and procrastinate on anger for a long, long time.

Absorbing God's Word implants in us His power to deliver us.

Respond promptly to God's Word, or suffer the consequences of self-deception.

God's word gives us our true identity. Responding to His word gives us strength.

Unguarded words cause our hearts to drift and makes shallow our faith.

True faith makes a difference in the lives of others.

Love and value your neighbor as you love and value yourself.

Prejudice violates the Royal Law of God's love.

Showing mercy to others reaps the same.

Phony faith is lifeless.

Authentic faith fosters life-giving results in us and those around us.

It's not faith or works; it's faith and works that please God.

Bridle the wild horses of your words, and you will mature your character.

Praising and cursing are not compatible with each other.

Advertise what God's doing in your life, but do it with the gentleness of wisdom.

Trouble results from jealous and self-serving hearts.

Godly wisdom is everything that worldly wisdom is not.

Asking God with pure motives puts us in sync with being God's friend.

Just say yes to opportunities, and then go do the right thing.

Living patient and expectant keeps hopes active and enduring.

Grumbling and complaining disguises the judgmental motives of the heart.

People of integrity are not prone to stumble into hypocrisy.

Pray for others first.

Go after those who wander from the wonder of God's truth.

HUMILITY OPENS THE CHANNEL FOR WISDOM

I begin with humility, I act with humility, I end with humility. Humility leads to clarity.
ERIC GREITENS

Asking for wisdom begins and ends with humility. In scattered times, we think that asking for wisdom is asking for something we don't deserve, don't yet have, or don't yet see. We think we're not worthy. That's not true. Jesus was made to us wisdom; therefore, it's not about us being worthy. Let's go on. Sometimes wisdom is something we do have but don't recognize. Other times, we act on wisdom without realizing it. That's grace. It's all grace. Because of His grace, the following holds true.

God is passionately invested in developing us into something we could never be without His direction and intervention.

Sometimes wisdom comes as a direction or an answer to prayer. I close this chapter with a simple example of practical wisdom that came from an answered prayer that JoAn and I prayed years ago. Remember James' words: 'If you lack wisdom, ask for it'? We asked.

Looking back now, I realize that earning my master's degree immediately after earning my bachelor's degree was God's wisdom in action. The longer that I'm on the planet, the more grateful I become of His wisdom. Who knew we would end up raising five children over the next twenty years. There never would have been a better time to pursue our education.

Here's the background information that led to this decision. JoAn and I prayed about two decisions. One was for me to get my masters, and another was for JoAn to become a trained nurse. At the time we prayed, I was in my final semester at William Carey College in Hattiesburg, Mississippi. In the next few months, I would graduate with a BA in theatre. We also believed we should relocate somewhere, but were clueless as to where. So, here's the simple prayer we prayed. We only prayed it once.

"If it's your will that Gene get a master's degree and that JoAn enroll in nursing school, please open a door."

And God did, but not as we expected. A few days after our prayer, the head of the theatre department at William Carey called me into his office and asked me to come on staff as an instructor. He encouraged me to work on my master's across town at the University of Southern Mississippi.

As we pursued this direction, we checked out a technical college for nursing only a couple of miles away. Next to that college was a daycare just right for our two-year old daughter, Laura. Additionally, the Dean of Women had an opening for dorm parents. She asked us to become dorm parents! A plus was that we could eat every meal in the college cafeteria for free. We wouldn't have to cook for the duration of our training!

Never have the pieces of a puzzle fell so perfectly in place. Here's what I've learned:

> **Wisdom is often the answer to a simple prayer prayed from the home base of humility.**

ABRAHAM'S WISDOM

Living in God's wisdom takes us forward. Abraham walked in a level of faith filled with wisdom. The book of Hebrews points out that Abraham carried himself forward by faith and never looked back.

> *Faith motivated Abraham to obey God's call and leave the familiar to discover the territory he was destined to inherit from God. So, he left with only a promise and without even knowing ahead of time where he was going, Abraham stepped out in faith.*
> HEBREWS 11:8

Later in the same chapter, verse 14:

> *For clearly, those who live this way are longing for the appearing of a heavenly city! And if their hearts were still remembering what they left behind, they would have found an opportunity to go back.*

God wants to be pursued. Pursuing God empties us of us! There is a part of us that tends to block the flow of his wisdom. We call it our unrenewed mind. The fact that Jesus grew in wisdom tells us that we, also, can grow in wisdom.

Jesus grew in stature, so do we. We know that is true. Jesus grew in favor exponentially among His followers. So, do we. But when it comes to wisdom, we tend to think Godly wisdom is only for the few. That line of thought falls out of line with more than just the scripture in Luke 2:52.

CAN WE GROW IN WISDOM?

Paul prayed that grace be multiplied to believers. If grace can be multiplied, what else can be multiplied? Can wisdom be multiplied? Yes, it can. God designed us to receive wisdom. Why is so much wisdom lacking in our world today? The simple answer is that the noise of our world drowns out the sound of Godly wisdom. What can we do? We have to go after it. Get aggressive. Go full throttle after wisdom. Toughen up our faith. Downsize our feelings. Pursue wisdom.

Proverbs 1:2 tells us that the book of Proverbs was written so we could **attain wisdom and discipline.** It's written so we can attain **understanding words of insight.** We must embrace God's intended purpose and wisdom for our lives. Here's an overview of the availability of wisdom.

Wisdom is loud & waiting to be heard: Proverbs 1:20-21 tells us wisdom is noisy. Wisdom raises her voice in the public squares and in the noisy streets, and in those gateways, she makes her speeches! Wisdom is not prone to hide. Wisdom is out there waiting to be found. Wisdom waits to be discerned.

What's the problem? Proverbs 2:2 tells us to 'turn our ear to wisdom!' And to 'apply our heart to understanding.' If we don't turn our ear to wisdom, our heart will not have anything to apply. It comes back to listening!

Wisdom is evident in people who have habitually turned their ear to hear wisdom's voice even in nosy public places. By the word wisdom, the Book of Proverbs includes natural and spiritual wisdom. We should seek out both. We have to be tough enough to do whatever it takes to prioritize hearing Godly wisdom.

Remember that when we go after Jesus, we're also going after all that He is as Father, Son, and Holy Spirit. I Corinthians 1:30 tells us that He has been made for us wisdom. Jesus has a voice in our lives. His voice is the Holy Spirit. He wants to be heard. We know that Faith comes by hearing. God expects us to be vigilant pursuers of Godly wisdom. He expects us to live tuned in to His wisdom. Pursuing His wisdom is pursuing Him.

Proverbs 2:10 says that **wisdom will enter your heart**! Our heart has to make room for wisdom. Defining our heart as our mind, will, and emotions, we come to understand why our heart is so crowded! Like hoarders of household goods, we hoard toxic thoughts and mindsets and emotional baggage. We have to delete data entries contrary to Godly wisdom. Just because we've always thought a certain way about our life or about the world that we live in does not justify giving those ways a foothold in our heart. Over the years we've lived on the planet, our heart becomes open game for whatever comes its way. We have to reestablish ourselves as the gatekeeper of what we hold in our hearts. We have to maintain the borders of our heart.

WISDOM HAS A PARTNER – UNDERSTANDING!

Proverbs 3:13 (NIV) says those who find wisdom are blessed; the same is true for those who gain understanding. Paul taught the early church to pray for the *spirit of wisdom and understanding* (Ephesians 1:17 (KJ)). We can have them both if we will go after them.

Proverbs 4, verse 7 (NIV) tells us that ***Wisdom is supreme, therefore get wisdom. Though it cost you all you have, get understanding.*** In Proverbs 7:4 (NIV), we are told to *talk to wisdom and call out to understanding.* In Proverbs 9:10 (NIV), we read: ***The fear of the Lord is the beginning of wisdom, and knowledge of the Holy One is understanding.*** It is on us to go after all that God has for us in this life. Obviously, we learn from the above scriptures that wisdom and understanding only require that we go after them. God is not hiding either one from us, but both for us. We just have to live in the hunt. Ask for both. Wisdom and understanding play well together. Whenever we gain wisdom, understanding is never too far away. It is expected that we grow, increase and develop in wisdom. Jesus did. He had to!

Does wisdom have a location? Proverbs 10:11 (NIV) **tells us that** *wisdom is found on the lips of the discerning.* Verse 14 tells us that *wise men store up knowledge* and verse 23 informs us that *a man of understanding delights in wisdom.* Both wisdom and understanding are connected. Find one and you'll find the other. God expects wisdom to flow from our mouth. How do I know? Verse 31 of this same chapter tells us that *the lips of the righteous brings forth wisdom.* We need to hear ourselves speak God's wisdom to ourselves.

What attracts Wisdom & Understanding? Proverbs 11:2 (NIV) confirms that with humility comes wisdom. Wisdom brings us praise (Proverbs 12:8 (NIV)). Proverbs 13:10 (NIV) tells us that *wisdom is found in those who take advice,* and the eighth verse in chapter 14 (NIV) informs us that *the wisdom of the prudent is to give thought to their ways.* Verse 33 concludes that *wisdom reposes in the heart of the discerning.* This is God's will.

If we are expected to have a relationship with wisdom based on the Old Covenant (scriptures from Proverbs), imagine how awesome wisdom and powerful it is in the New Covenant. Paul tells us that in Christ we have a better covenant. That means we have better access to wisdom because Jesus was made to us wisdom! How much greater should wisdom's influence be in our relationship with Jesus through the Holy Spirit? The Holy Spirit teaches us. It's a slam dunk when we live teachable with the *teacher,* the Holy Spirit! Being teachable attracts God's wisdom and understanding.

Wisdom has advantages! In Proverbs 19:8 (NKJV), we learn that *He who gets wisdom loves his own soul; he who cherishes understanding prospers.* And in verse 11 of this same chapter, the writer says this: *A man's wisdom gives him patience; it is to his glory to overlook an offense.*

Wisdom is not an elusive trait that God hides from us. Wisdom is a treasure we already have in Jesus. We don't have to allow the devil or unfamiliar seasons to sidetrack us from God's intended relationship. We don't have to wander from the wonder of God. God calls us to find wisdom in our relationship with Jesus.

THE CHALLENGE

I grew up believing wisdom was for the elite. I believed great opportunities came only to those who lived across town not on our dirt road. I thought everything in my life would be based on where I came from. Not true. Not true. Not true. Wisdom is for those who seek it, ask for it, expect it.

As reborn believers, we should be dancing circles around wisdom. What is wrong with our world? More to the point is the fact that our world is less when we are not fully engaged in Godly wisdom. Without His wisdom, we're never fully engaged. Our relationships are less, our life's work is less, and our impact is certainly less. Distracted, we grow overwhelmed. Our intercourse with the world's conversation tends to become more reflective of their ways of processing life. But there is a way out. Wisdom beyond our years, beyond our education, and beyond our relationships is available for the asking.

> *And now out of his fullness we are fulfilled!*
> JOHN 1:16

Our fulfillment comes from His presence. It is not the wisdom of this world that Paul preached. He says in his first letter to the Corinthians:

> *The message I preached and how I preached it was not an attempt to sway you with persuasive arguments but to prove to you the almighty power of God's Holy Spirit. For God intended that your faith not be established on man's wisdom but by trusting in his almighty power.*
> I CORINTHIANS 2:4-5

Jesus grew in wisdom. Let's follow His life by focusing on the wise decisions that positioned Him to fulfill His calling and purpose. Let's start at the very beginning of what we know about Him beyond the crib. Here's a quick look at the progress and growth of wisdom in the life of Jesus.

JESUS' LIFE OF WISDOM.

He played what He knew against the experts of His day. In His childhood adventure, He was so caught up in the discussions with the religious leaders that He lost track of time. Oblivious to His parents search for Him, He exhausted the knowledge of the temple leaders. He had a sense of what Martin Luther King described as the 'fierce urgency of now'! Every day mattered to Him. Every day must matter to us, as well.

Jesus' hunger for wisdom prompted him for nightly conversations with His Father. There He grew in wisdom beyond His culture and times. Yes, He knew why He was on the planet, but His hunger drove Him to midnight hours of intimacy with the only one who had the wisdom for which He hungered, His Heavenly Father.

JESUS SOUGHT OUT THE GREATEST INFLUENCER OF THE TIMES.

He connected with John the Baptist, who was not only His cousin but the greatest influencer and most controversial character in the culture He lived. Certainly, it was out of obedience that Jesus insisted that John baptize Him, but there was another connection on a more basic level as well. John was a standout. He had generated a buzz that social media of our day would have found captivating. Jesus' brief moment with John touched a common gift that they both shared. Their prophetic influence went beyond the norm of the day. They both lived in the 'fierce urgency of now'!

John carved out his existence and influence as a groundbreaker. Jesus would do the same. That day in the Jordan was their moment. The baptism of Jesus confirmed to John his own faithfulness as the trailblazer preceding the Messiah. It was a holy moment for both. John watched in awe as the Holy Spirit anointed Jesus. He had known that one day he would see the Holy Spirit descend like a dove on the redeemer of mankind. His hunger for that moment had kept him focused. That hunger gave him the stamina to be the influencer in the wilderness. His popularity had touched everyone from commoner to royalty. But from that day on, John yielded his influence for the one he recognized publicly as the Lamb of God. John would decrease. Christ would increase. That was John's wisdom from the Holy Spirit. It was also the wisdom Jesus embraced.

JESUS REFUSED SATAN'S ATTEMPTS TO MARGINALIZE HIS PURPOSE.

Everyone has a proving ground—the wilderness was Jesus'. He knew who He was up against. He knew what He was fighting for. The wisdom of His Father's words was His weapon of choice. Jesus returned from the wilderness empowered. The next three years would be a battle, but the prophetic wisdom of His Father's words kept Him empowered to redeem mankind. His daily pursuit of intimacy with His Father kept him effectively navigating His purpose through spiritual wilderness of the day.

JESUS' WISDOM GREW IN PARTNERSHIP WITH FOLLOWERS.

Traveling the country with a team of novices marked the life of Jesus. He enjoyed a continual ground swell of influence and responsibility. In one-on-one efforts outside their comfort zone, His followers' influence grew in proportion to how they grew in Godly wisdom. Jesus immediately began building a team. He traveled the country moving in and out of the acceptable and unacceptable people groups of the day. He took His ministry beyond the cultural ways of His hometown. Following closely in His shadow were the vagabond travelers known as disciples. They learned how Jesus leveraged opportunities. They learned to see unexpected modes of operation. They defied the odds and became world changers. Jesus discipled them in a world whose substance was lacking and whose permanence had a shelf life near extinction. He shared His wisdom.

JESUS' WISDOM IN GETHSEMANE

The collision of forces, both spiritual and natural, became volcanic in the Garden of Gethsemane. As expected, the disciples fell asleep. They couldn't be counted on. Jesus, all alone, dealt with the last ounce of His humanity's emotions. His love for His followers sleeping in the garden clashed with wisdom's mandate to take Him to the cross for their salvation. The wisdom of His Father's mandate bore down on Him to go the distance. To say those hours in the garden were difficult is to minimize the conflict raging within Him.

Wisdom had to win the day in the temporary shadow of defeat. His tear-stained life positioned itself in the crosshairs of His Father's wisdom and the world's hatred. Everything led to this test. On this earth, there is always another test. There is always another encounter with something greater than our individual preferences. There comes a place in every life where wisdom must win the day in unfamiliar places. We must yield to that moment, because in the death of what matters in our natural world is the birth of something that matters greater in God's eternal. On a much smaller scale such moments come to us daily. This taking hold of something greater while letting go of something lesser is wisdom's intentional advantage. We have to see it. We have to face it. We have to embrace it. We have to allow it. Wisdom reveals itself exponentially in those moments. Leveraging those moments with others watching brings unexpected wisdom for the moments we are yet to live.

JESUS' WISDOM BEYOND THE GRAVE.

The greatest depth of wisdom walks us out of circumstances where everything seems hopeless. Jesus did. This level of wisdom rushes in with the faithfulness of God as our finisher. He is the closer! He wins the game for us. Wisdom's scent defeats the smell of death. Wisdom's supreme moment is where everything scattered comes back together. Victory is won through the resurrection power of wisdom. Wisdom always declares 'there is a lifting'!

Ultimately this moment transcends logic. Wisdom and Grace morph the moment beyond our natural expectations. This is the life supernatural wisdom lives. Wisdom at this level supersedes the agony of all previous hunger pains, influences, temptations, partnerships and Gethsemane type moments. Wisdom's relationship to us becomes ongoing when our surrender to God's will becomes non-negotiable.

God outsmarted Satan with redemption through the foolishness of the cross. God's wisdom was on full display at Calvary. His wisdom still trumps any efforts of Satan. James' letter lays bare the excuses we often evoke for living a subpar existence. But since wisdom is the principal thing, what if we make it the principle thing God intended. What if we leverage wisdom and stretch toward the high calling of God in Christ Jesus? What if we stretch our responses to life beyond the typical banter of the world? What if we ask expectantly for the full measure of wisdom as God has promised? What if, with Godly wisdom, we leverage life against the scheme of distractions in the scattered times we live?

9

THE REACHING OUT PRINCIPLE

Our calling in life doesn't change just because our circumstances do!

WORDS & DOORS

Sitting in a dark and damp prison doesn't strike us as a starting place to pen a large portion of the New Testament, but prison was Paul's starting place. Chained to guards, Paul was almost immoveable. Prison had become his new normal.

The correlation here is that sometimes a change in our circumstances can leave us feeling confined. Have you ever felt restricted, boxed in, trapped? Ever felt confined to a season of life that you thought would never end? Most of us have.

Words! Aren't they always our challenge? How to open the conversation? How to make the connection? How to keep it real? But let's get real. When life gets tough, we tend to turn inward, not outward. We rarely see tough times as the best time to reach out and help others.

In the following exerts from Paul's writing, note the following themes: **Open Doors, Words, and Reaching Out!**

And please pray for me, <u>that God will open a door of opportunity</u> for us to preach the revelation of the mystery of Christ for whose sake I am imprisoned. Pray that I would unfold and reveal fully this mystery, for that is my delightful assignment.

COLOSSIANS 4:3-4

'<u>that whenever I speak, words may be given me</u> so that I will fearlessly make known the mystery of the gospel, for which I am an ambassador in chains. Pray that I may declare it fearlessly, as I should.'

EPHESIANS 6:20-21 (NIV)

Strength comes from reaching outwardly. Paul proved this. In prison, he kept his perspective in the context of the bigger picture. His drug of choice, if you will, was sharing the Gospel and its power to transform lives! Our calling in life doesn't change just because our circumstances do! Sitting in a dark and stifling prison, Paul preached the Gospel to his audience – the Roman guards! His boldness and anointing worked even there. Our uniqueness and strengths are not confined to what's happening on the outside of us. Leveraging opportunities to strengthen others is life-giving. Our strengths have to find a way to express themselves for the benefit of others. Like flood waters finding avenues to flow, we have to find avenues where our strengths can flow. Do you remember from previous chapters that everyone has God-given strengths? We also have a bias to use them. Reaching out leverages our strengths for the benefit of others. As we give strength, we receive strength, even in scattered times.

A friend of mine spent more than ten years in prison due to false charges and a trumped verdict. You'll read her amazing story in the last chapter. Imagine knowing you are innocent and yet living in solitary confinement! Yet she found a way to be who she really was in the darkness around her. Like Paul, it became her choice to reach out. The same is true for us. It is our choice to decide whether to be a reservoir of regrets, disappointments, and depression or to be the river that finds the outlet to be who God made us.

Paul found that leveraging God's grace kept him resilient. He learned that when grace runs deep, doors open and words come. That's why they were Paul's number one prayer request. He wanted others to learn the same. Paul knew that if life became only about him and the conversations recycling in his head, his life would become a stagnant reservoir and nothing more. He had to find ways to reach out. He lived radar-focused on finding the right words to minister to others. He lived ready when doors opened. Sometimes he opened them with his words!

No doubt the words Paul spoke to his Roman guards opened a world beyond them. Writing letters became the outlet of a lifetime. He became a wordsmith. A wordsmith is one who searches and chisels the right words into powerful sentences. In Paul's case, he searched for the right words to write powerful letters. He documented the struggles and triumphs of the early church. His letters have provided generations he never met with the Words of God that open doors today for understanding and revelation. Leveraging opportunities to reach out and strengthen others when our life gets scattered is a game changer.

REACHING OUT RESOLUTELY TURNS US

I yearn to come and be face-to-face with you and get to know you. For I long to impart to you some spiritual gift that will empower you to stand strong in your faith. Now, this means that when we come together and are side by side, something wonderful will be released. We can expect to be co-encouraged and co-comforted by each other's faith.

ROMANS 1:11-12

Where does reaching out begin? You're probably thinking of getting close geographically or socially. Wrong! Look no further than about 11 inches below your mouth. Reaching out begins in our heart. The Holy Spirit knows how to rein us in and turn us outwardly in our thought life. The thoughts behind Paul's letter to the Ephesians came to him as he stared at the armor confining him. It was the Holy Spirit that gave him the words we find translated in the King James Bible that read:

We wrestle not against flesh and blood, but against principalities, against powers, against rulers of the darkness of this world, against spiritual wickedness in high places.

EPHESIANS 6:12 (KJV)

The Holy Spirit knows how to unfold to us the inward needs of those around us. We're surrounded by people in a fight, wrestling against the odds. Armed with the mind of Christ, we become laser focused on the words and actions needed. Physical needs are the obvious needs. Spiritual needs go deeper. Every word counts.

Mobilize the Word of God. In granting honorary American citizenship to Winston Churchill in1963, President Kennedy said that Churchill 'mobilized the English language and sent it into battle'! He was quoting Edward Murrow's words spoken during WWII regarding Churchill's leadership against the forces of the Nazi march across Europe. A similar thought should be our thought. As believers, we should engage in *mobilizing the Word* of God by sending it into battle for the needs of those beyond our scattered thinking and circumstances. We need to trust the Holy Spirit for the right words in our heart. Why? Because that is where reaching out begins. In our heart and in the words that rise, we speak. Doors open.

Paul wrote to the Roman believers his desire to come and *establish* them. The word 'establish' in Romans 1:11 (KJV) comes from a Greek word meaning 'to turn you in a certain direction'. As God continues to establish us in the faith, we should recognize He is always turning us in a certain direction. That direction ultimately is outward. Here's how Paul worded this verse:

> *For I long to see you, that I may impart unto you some spiritual gift, to the end ye may be established.*
> ROMANS 1:11 (KJV)

The right words turn our hearts in a certain direction. They anchor us to the absolutes of our faith. Thinking and meditating on God's Word turns us in the direction of our calling and opportunities to meet the needs around us. Paul's fulfillment was in reaching out to the early church. He longed to steady their faith. He lived to connect with them in order to turn them to the one who could stabilize their faith. He lived out Gods' Word on a grand scale. We can do the same. Reaching out is always part of the grand scale of what God is doing on the earth today. It is the part we play. Satan loves to get us sidetracked. But what turns us, what establishes us, are God's words in our heart. Reaching out resolutely turns us beyond our preference for the familiar. Don't live closed minded to adventures in unfamiliar places when the door opens.

DOORS

The Church is not a once a week service. That's a gathering. Reaching out is not simply about living outsider-focused rather than insider-focused. There's more to it. Reaching out is about living life out loud, regardless of the personal stuff we're going through.

Paul writes to the Corinthian church:

> *Now, it's because of God's mercy that we have been entrusted with the privilege of this new covenant ministry. And we will not quit or faint with weariness.*
> II CORINTHIANS 4:1

Our generosity to reach out is God's mercy in action, and mercy is the base of operation in reaching out. Mercy has a way of extending the boundaries of our lives. Mercy reaches beyond those who deserve mercy. We know that from personal experience. Right? That's where God found us. That undeserving revelation that God's love could not be earned. That place we call grace. That place where mercy came running after us.

Jesus never stepped into the presence of anyone who deserved His mercy or love. Love motivated Him. Grace carried Him. Mercy identified Him. He lived prompted by the Holy Spirit's presence. Reaching out is never limited to reaching people who we think deserve God's mercy. The target audience of mercy is always on the crowd of undeserving people. Mercy has a big target audience.

When Jesus dined at Matthew the tax collector's house, He enjoyed the company of society's outcast. He was fearless. He depended on the Holy Spirit for the right words. Words came easily for Jesus when He extended mercy to outcasts. Eventually, He had to find the right words to respond to the Pharisees.

The Pharisees questioned the appropriateness of Jesus enjoying the company of such low-life people as Matthew's circle of friends. His well worded response should be our mandate in reaching out. Jesus said, 'healthy people don't need to see a doctor, but the sick will go for treatment' (Matthew 9:12). Verse 13 conflicts with our tendency to prefer comfort in trying times.

> *Then he added, Now you should go and study the meaning of the verse: I want you to show mercy, not just offer me sacrifice. For I have come to invite the outcasts of society and sinners, not those who think they are already on the right path.*
>
> MATTHEW 9:13

Jesus' ministry touched every fragment of society. He lived responsive to those who needed His Father's mercy. In fact, a quick study of Jesus' miracles reveals an assortment of people usually kicked to the curb of society. They came to him crying for mercy, and He responded with mercy. That's what we can do.

Friends of mine in Lethbridge, Alberta, Canada, minister daily to people on the street who are homeless and/or addicted to substances. This ministry is called Streets Alive, and their congregation is street people. Street people carry their life's possessions in a backpack. That's all they own. They've been kicked to the curb through a variety of circumstances. Regardless of how they got there, these people need mercy. Streets Alive began when someone years ago decided to reach out. Not everyone ends up ministering on the streets of the world to those who have literally been kicked to the curb. The average person avoids making eye contact with street people. But that's one thing that everyone can do to give them a sense of dignity. In fact, a smile may be even better. The congregation of Streets Alive needs mercy as much as the next guy. Mercy knows no class distinctions. We all need mercy.

Jesus lived in the rush hour chaos of His three-year journey to the cross. What stopped Him in His tracks should stop us. He saw no limitations between talking with a Samaritan woman at a well than He saw in feeding thousands of people on a hillside. He saw potential in opportunities that His followers walked past. He heard cries for mercy that others tried to silence. Extending mercy strengthened Him. When the disciples were beside themselves at the sight of Jesus talking with the Samaritan woman at the well, He spoke of a nourishment to which they were clueless.

JESUS REACHED OUT TO SATISFY A KINGDOM AGENDA

Less you think I'm just referring to people in dire situations, allow me to broaden the subject. Take another look at Jesus reaching out. This story is found in Luke 5:1-10 and it has nothing to do with people kicked to the curb of society. Instead, Jesus reaches out strategically for Kingdom purposes under the guise of teaching the crowd. Here's my take on what was really happening that day.

Peter and his partners had fished all night, again. They were on the beach cleaning their nets when Jesus and the crowd came waltzing down the shoreline toward them. Peter and his partners' night of fishing had produced zero results. They weren't cleaning their nets of fish!

The crowd following Jesus, like a big catch of fish, were caught up in the net of his teaching. The crowd crowded closer and closer. They grew larger and larger.

Peter saw them coming. It's embarrassing enough to be cleaning empty nets any time, but to be doing it with a crowd of spectators following Jesus was even worse. Nowhere to run, nowhere to hide. Peter pushed on with his net cleaning until, that is, Jesus jumped into his boat. Jesus could have jumped into any of the boats gathered there that morning. But Jesus was strategic. His brand of reaching out that morning was a matter of Kingdom business. This tired and weary, fishless, water soaked, future apostle of the first century church kindly obliged to push his boat out a little deeper into the water. The crowd gathered around to listen and maybe see a miracle or two.

We don't know what Jesus taught that morning. Certainly, Peter listened intently as did the rest of his partners. We know this because we've read the end of the story where they left everything and took off following Jesus in the grand scheme of Kingdom business. But let's back up and drill down on the reaching out techniques in this story.

No one was kicked to the curb that day. Jesus was fulfilling His purpose on earth as much as He was reaching out. He always was doing both—so should we! His teaching that day stirred up something at the core of Peter's heart. Something was missing. It wasn't just the failure of their night's fishing that Jesus was touching with His teaching. Peter's life was on the edge. His family's business had always been fishing. He knew nothing else, except he knew something else was missing. There was a place in his heart that was incomplete. His day-in and day-out routine wasn't satisfying and not just when his nightly catch was zero.

Jesus' teaching ended and He turned to Peter with a directive that tested a stubborn place in Peter's heart. We all have a place like that. But everything Jesus taught that day had already stirred Peter's heart. Jesus directive was more of a command: 'Row out into the deep water'. Peter heard it as repetitious of what he had been doing all night! Isn't that sometimes God's directive to us? 'Just keep doing what you've been doing'. It keeps us in the game even when we aren't sure what the game is! Peter reluctantly launches his boat out into the water, but not before letting Jesus know that he's only doing it because Jesus told him to! Precisely what Jesus hoped to hear. Why?

Jesus confirmed that day in His future apostle's heart the measure of obedience He was looking for. To the outside world, Peter's future as an apostle didn't make common sense. But, nothing about Peter's adventure in life would be common. You know the rest of the story. That day at the beach Peter had to signal for his partners to help him. Their catch of fish that day surpassed the number anyone had ever caught in one day.

The crowd watched the story unfold. Peter and the gang were having the time of their life. Their catch, according to the research I've done, numbered to the equivalent of an entire weeks' catch. Nearly a million fish got caught up in that harvest from the Galilean waters! Peter's response? 'Go away from me, I'm a sinful man'! The tension between where Peter thought his life would go and where Jesus would take it intensified. The awestruck crowd focused on the catch of fish. Jesus focused on the catch of apostles! Jesus tells Peter in verse 10:

> *'Do not yield to fear. From now on you'll catch men for salvation'*

The Sea of Galilee was the setting that day for the launch of ministries that would change the world. Today the Sea of Galilee is seven miles wide and 12.5 miles long. Imagine, on the day I'm referencing in this chapter, Jesus found Peter among the 87.5 square miles of water! Imagine who God can find through your life. Imagine! Distance is nothing to God. Our partnership with the Holy Spirit shrinks the distances between the relevance needed and the people who need it. A life without fear is a life without boundaries. When we leave every option on the table for God to use, we live outwardly focused. Again, that's where the magic happens. That's where mercy travels.

Jesus' words touched a soft spot in Peter's heart. Peter was prone to give in to fear and inferiority! Take a fuller look at Peter's life a few years later, and it comes full circle. What motivated Peter to deny Jesus? Fear! But greater than Peter's fearful nature, Jesus tapped into the strength Peter would bring to the Gospel: Obedience! Jesus confirmed the depth of obedience that was in Peter. Peter didn't know it, His partners didn't see it, but Jesus would draw it out. Peter just knew that whatever Jesus' words to him would be, he would obey! Mission accomplished.

There's something refreshing about coming to the water's edge of opportunity and stepping into the boat of someone else' circumstances. Reaching out is often a matter of helping someone discover what is in them. Tapping into the strengths in another person's life is monumental. Look for people who are as curious as Peter and his gang. Sometimes it's God's strategic plan to connect us with them. Reaching them is as impactful as performing a miracle, because in some way, impacting a curious heart is a miracle. Expect your uniqueness to make a difference. When your unique strengths impact the release of the strengths in others, it's a Kingdom thing!

Reaching out to pull to the forefront something so subtle as 'obedience' was Jesus' strategy that day. Reaching out will take you there for the sake of helping others uncover strengths hidden by the struggles in their heart. Everyone has a soft spot that Jesus' words can touch. Encourage yourself to live curiously engaged in the tactical strategies of the Holy Spirit. Keep yourself promptly listening.

Working your way through this eight-letter acronym will bring the point home. It illustrates how God is always working to open doors. Reaching out re-orients, engages, awakens, challenges, humbles, invests, nourishes, and graces our life.

8 BENEFITS FROM REACHING OUT TO OTHERS – REACHING OUT

R - RE-ORIENTS US

James 1:27 commands us to be doers of the Word, not just hearers. We are purposed to be distributors in life not reservoirs of cataloged experience and information. *Reaching out re-orients us to a fuller perspective of the world around us and a fuller perception of ourselves in that world.*

E - ENGAGES US

Once we are re-oriented to the world around us, engaging initiates an even deeper experience. Here's a simple truth I've taught students for years:

> **You have to connect with others so there can be a conversation and so there can be a conversion and eventually a collaboration.**

> **Connect + Converse + Convert + Collaborate**

Why? Because conversations don't just happen. People have to connect. If you're at a coffee shop and watch people walk in and immediately jump into animated conversations, it's because they have a long history of connecting with each other. Connecting is intentional. When conversations pull from us information that we don't know we know, engagement goes into overdrive. Suddenly we are engaged in subject matter separate from the transitional moment we're living. This level of communion pulls from us. We learn to pull from others by asking the right questions in order to engage them in healthy conversations. Why? So that God can use us to add value to them, and we awaken!

A - AWAKENS US

Reaching out is powerful because it not only re-orients us and engages us, but it awakens us to the needs of others. The engagement of reaching out adds value to others and teaches us how to connect with perfect strangers. We learn to add intentional value spontaneously. Reaching out broadens our world view and refreshes us. And then, reaching out challenges us.

C - CHALLENGES US

We don't know everything. We quickly encounter people and situations that are beyond our pay grade. Challenges beyond our expertise and experience pushes us to finds ways to meet the needs around us. We either encourage them to find ways to connect with better resources, or we learn to step further and further beyond what we know. We become resourceful for others. We flip the switch from what's been consuming us. We dig deeper.

H - HUMBLES US

It's humbling to embrace that there are seasons when relationships run their course. The intensity of the collaborations we establish must be flexible enough that anyone can move on to their next season without us! I'm not saying that there are no life-long friendships that defy seasons. But, to be honest, your inner circle of relationships has probably changed over the years. You must be humble enough to let go and reach out to new people and experiences.

I - INVESTS US

Investing in ourselves equips us for future collaborations. Stagnation results when we allow the absence of fresh information and revelation. If nothing fresh is flowing in us emotionally, intellectually, or spiritually, we become stagnate. Stagnation leads us back to isolation. When all we talk about is what we're going through, our conversations become inwardly focused and self-serving. Investing is about others.

N - NURTURES US

Exhausted, Jesus sat down by a well. A woman came to routinely draw water. It seemed an odd time of day to Him. He leaned into a conversation with a complete stranger. He connected with her first over the subject of water. The conversation shifted quickly, and there was an instant conversion of her trust in this stranger from Galilee. She eventually ran back into town and brought out her friends. The collaboration that followed changed lives. Jesus hung around for hours that day. He said the experience nurtured Him. Jesus said: 'My nourishment comes from doing my Father's will.' He taught His disciples the nurturing nature of reaching outside themselves. The same is true for us.

G - GRACES US

Grace and Truth came to earth through Jesus Christ. He flowed with it. His life reached out 24/7 to a smorgasbord of personalities and needs. His grace made them receptive to faith. Those that refused to receive didn't get it. The same is true for us. It takes grace to remember and release the life-giving substance within us. Never separate grace from truth. Truth alone will enslave you. Walking in truth requires grace. Together they transition us. The Greek word translated 'grace' comes from the word 'charis'. Here's the meaning from the Strong's Concordance:

Grace - God's divine influence on the heart and it's reflection in the life.

Living under the divine influence of God's grace should be reflective in our life. It is that reflection that moves us to reach outside of ourselves.

INSTINCTIVELY CREATIVE & COURAGEOUS PEOPLE EXCEED THE PERIMETERS OF WHERE THEY'VE BEEN
CARL LENZ,
HILLSONG CHURCH PASTOR, NEW YORK CITY

Never underestimate what you may think is insignificant or off limits for the Holy Spirit's intentions. Fear is a curb the devil loves to kick people against. Fear is restrictive. Those who reach out must fight that fear; that baseline of dread. Dreading to face life full front is a strategy of the devil. Reluctance is a kissing cousin to dread. We have ways of talking ourselves out of reaching out, especially when our life gets scattered.

If you've never read Carl Lenz' book "Own the Moment", I highly recommend it. He practices creative courage on the streets of New York City. Lenz does it through what James calls the 'Royal Law". Let's go there.

THE COURAGEOUS ROAR OF MERCY

In the childhood favorite, The Wizard of Ox, we sympathize with the lion who has lost his courage. His roar had been silenced. That's the strategy of the devil. He plots to silence our roar! This point gains clarity when we look deeper into Psalm 103:1-5. You may know this among all the favorite verses in your life. Verse 5 came alive to me when ministering 25 years ago.

> *...Who satisfies your mouth with good things. So that your youth is renewed like the eagle's.*
> PSALM 103:5 (KJV)

First thing we articulate when an opportunity to reach out comes knocking at our door is the thought that we won't know what to say! But the psalmist declares in this psalm that one of the benefits of being blessed is that God 'satisfies our mouth with good things.' That means God promises to fill our mouth with life-giving words. The second truth here is a little more subtle. Usually we get so caught up in being like the eagle that we miss the 'youth is renewed' part. Oddly enough, when I first researched the meaning of the word youth, I discovered in its primitive root the idea of a lion's roar! When connecting that idea to the word youth, I came to the following conclusion.

One of God's great benefits is to keep us charged up and courageous with our faith. How? By supplying us with His words that roar with authority. Teenagers are always in a roar as they discover the fountain of their youthful potential. Having pastored youth in multiple generations, I've heard their roar many times. Their enthusiasm at discovering and acting as young persons on the move becomes a courageous roar! What a treasure that roar is. Boldness and curiosity run like wildfire through any teenage crowd when faith is at the center of it. Revival always has a roar quality.

Our boldness to reach out with confidence of heart as well as with words is liberating. Jesus jumps on the concept of courage. Jesus said:

And everything I've taught you is so that the peace which is in me will be in you and will give you great confidence as you rest in me. For in this unbelieving world you will experience trouble and sorrows, but you must be courageous, for I have conquered the world!

JOHN 16:33

Jesus declares both peace and courage. They are ours. But when intimidation (fear) rules our day, who we really are and what we have in Christ gets muffled. Intimidation distorts God's intentions. Reaching out and into the culture of our day becomes a challenge until we override our fear with God-given courage. Launching an attack on unbelievers in social media is not prudent nor courageous. Our courage should be an extension of Christ's love and mercy, not an extension of religion's judgmental ways.

Secondly, the Royal Law of Love focuses on valuing others not just loosely loving them.

Your calling is to fulfill the royal law of love as given to us in this Scripture: 'You must love and value your neighbor as you love and value yourself! For keeping this law is the noble way to live.'

JAMES 2:8

At age 20, I came alive to the power of God. I made Jesus Lord, not just Savior. There is a quantum leap of courage in that one statement. I found that courage is a learned response to life based on the vitality of God's Word within me. It is God's intention that every believer be courageous in walking out who Jesus is in their life. Making Jesus Lord is powerful.

This is the intent of reaching out: Love, Mercy and Courage! They are team players activated to empower others with God's truth. It is simply the extension of our relationship with Jesus made public that reaching out becomes emboldened. I challenge you to live as a courageous roar of God's mercy.

10

THE EXPECTATION PRINCIPLE

Expectancy is the atmosphere of miracles.
—Ed Cole

STARTING OVER

Scattered times are the setting of James' letter to those who had been dispersed by religious persecution. Suddenly for them, nothing seemed familiar: not the land, not the people, not their homes, nothing! But this sense of being scattered went deeper. The predictability on which their life's decisions had been made was also scattered. Adjustment to their new land included adjusting their emotional response to new surroundings and the people that inhabited that land. If you've experienced a major geographic move, you know what happens. Familiar friends elsewhere have gone on with their lives without you. Their familiar voices are slowly silenced by time and distance. You feel emotionally, mentally, and even spiritually separated from them, not just geographically relocated! We like predictability. In fact, predictability is like our security blanket. But in transitions, as when a baby's security blanket is in the wash, predictability goes missing in action.

In tough times, the predictability of our reality can come up short. We buy into a deranged version of God's perspective of our immediate. There is no welcome center that can reorient us because we feel torn from our previous familiar, not just relocated. We live so occupied by yesterday's expectations that we lack the fortitude to start over. We're in between places. No one calls out our name. We're tormented at the sight of faces that look familiar to those we miss, but really aren't.

> **It's not so much that we're afraid of change or so in love with old ways, but it's that place in between that we fear...It's like being between trapezes. There's nothing to hold on to.**
>
> MARILYN FERGUSON

It's what we know, not just who we know that will take us through difficulties. It matters what we believe about Jesus and what He has promised. James' experience with Jesus as His savior is what's on display here. Jesus said that we can know truth and truth sets us free.

> *Jesus said to those Jews who believed in him, "When you continue to embrace all that I teach, you prove that you are my true followers. For if you embrace the truth, it will release true freedom into your lives."*
>
> JOHN 8:31-32

Truth does not set us free from temptations nor tough times—both will exist as long as we're on earth—but truth can also set us free from ignorance of the truth we need to embrace in scattered times.

'... I'm writing to all the twelve tribes of Israel who have been sown as seeds among the nations'.

JAMES 1:1

The Good News is God is not limited by what limits us. He remains passionately invested in us, even when we're not. The God who brought Moses back from the dark side of the desert knows our name. He works behind the scenes connecting factors that will enrich our lives. He initiates random connections and cross pollenates narratives to create a new narrative in our heart. The gravitational pull of the future slowly draws us into a new journey. People introduce themselves, and we struggle to identify ourselves beyond what used to be us. Our expectations are so tied to our yesterday that detaching from it seems impossible. But in time we begin to explore new expectations. Our identity in this new place formulates. The dialogue in our mind broadens beyond the shadow of our past. It takes more than just time!

GOD'S KINGDOM NARRATIVE

As believers, we realize that God is always focused on a Kingdom narrative. Every major player in scripture found this truth to hold true. Moses on the backside of the desert adjusted to a life void of his royal upbringing. No one in the desert cared where he had really come from. His Egyptian leadership skills were of minimal consideration. God patiently refined Moses so he had an authoritative voice. His past was severed as God carried him into an unfamiliar land. In the wilderness, Moses' expectations were minimized. His responsibility was minimal as well. But all that would eventually change.

Flash forward forty years, and Moses' curiosity of a bush ablaze would spark an adventure he didn't see coming. God knows how to connect us to His purpose by what draws our curiosity. Moses' first assignment wasn't to deliver the Hebrew people. His first assignment was to see himself as a deliverer. He had to put himself out there. He had to call himself what God called him. He didn't go from backside of the desert to court side of the Egyptian hierarchy overnight. His expectations had to be forced into overdrive. But it began with how he saw himself. His expectations had to be fabricated in the desert, before God could materialize them in Pharaoh's court.

Moses' expectations had to find their truth in who God said he was. Moses asked, 'Who should I say sends me?' And God's reply was classic God: 'I am that I am'! God needs no back and forth to assure Himself of what He already knows is in us. It's just that we don't know what's in us. We don't know what we were born to do beyond scattered times.

Our expectations have to catch up. Moses had to call himself deliverer. In scattered times, we have to call ourselves as God sees us. We have to buy into the Kingdom narrative that is bigger than our individual moment. Otherwise, we'll buy into a twisted perspective of ourselves. If our discernment gets twisted, we'll voice a deranged narrative.

James' letter gives us specific directions. He cuts us no slack. Time in the Word rather than in our worries is priority number one. We have to grasp at every straw given to us by the Holy Spirit. We must hold ourselves responsible for rekindling the fire of God's expectations. Remember the *bushfire* in the wilderness that caught Moses' eye. Follow through with moments like these when God's presence is ablaze. Remember them. Build on them. Rehearse them over and over. Live out those times to stabilize your faith.

Here's how James put it to the scattered believers:

If you listen to the Word and don't live out the message you hear, you become like the person who looks in the mirror of the Word to discover the reflection of his face in the beginning. You perceive how God sees you in the mirror of the Word, but then you go out and forget your divine origin. But those who set their gaze deeply into the perfecting law of liberty are fascinated by and respond to the truth they hear and are strengthened by it – they experience God's blessing in all they do!

JAMES 1:23-25

Remembering is powerful, and expectations continually reshape the arc of our faith. Those Old Testament heroes understood this. The recollection of their exploits as recorded in the Book of Hebrews are preceded by the most famous verse in Hebrews 11.

Now faith brings our hopes into reality and becomes the foundation needed to acquire the things we long for. It is all the evidence required to prove what is still unseen. This testimony of faith is what previous generations were commended for. Faith empowers us to see that the universe was created and beautifully coordinated by the power of God's words! He spoke and the invisible realm gave birth to all that is seen.

HEBREW 11:1-3

Faith brings hope. Hope translates into expectations. Expectations are anchored in what we really believe. Moses had to wrestle with this truth.

Imagine that instead of confronting Pharaoh to let 'his people go,' Moses had just sat around in Egypt reminiscing about life in the wilderness? Imagine if David, after killing Goliath, had lived his life telling shepherd stories! They both had a common background that could have pulled them backward. Lessons from our past are meant to move us forward. But, expectations from our past have to be re-edited by the Kingdom dialogue of God for our future.

MOVING FORWARD

The first few verses in James' letter probably caused those early Christians a bit of whiplash. Wrapping their minds around what James was proposing would take some time. His opening challenge touched more than their nerves. James touched their hearts with directives to move them forward. But there was a cost they had to be willing to pay. Moving forward always extracts a cost. Rekindling our expectations also comes with a cost. Cost, being what it is, requires us to do whatever it takes to move forward. But by not giving up what we know, we can embrace what James says in his letter:

> *For you know that when your faith is tested it stirs up power within you to endure all things.*
>
> JAMES 1:3

James helps us recognize the power within us by showing us eight powerful expectations in his letter.

8 EXPECTATIONS

HERE ARE THE EXPECTATIONS LAID OUT IN JAMES' EPISTLE
- **Character Refinement** (James 1:2-4)
- **Absorption of the Word of God** (James 1:19-22)
- **Dominion over Judgment** (James 2:12-13)
- **Self-Control** (James 3:2)

- **Godly Wisdom** (James 1:5)
- **Standing Firm against the Devil** (James 4:5-8)
- **God's Relationship Becoming More Intimate** (James 4:5-8)
- **Harvest** (James 1:25; 3:17-18)

Let's break them down.

EXPECTATION #1: CHARACTER REFINEMENT

God's character emerges in us as He passionately invests in us. He develops us into someone we could never be without His direction and intervention. His intervention firmly moves to refine our character in line with His purpose. Remember what Paul wrote to the Philippian Church?

> *Therefore, my dear friends, as you have always obeyed – not only in my presence, but now much more in my absence – continue to work out your salvation with fear and trembling, for it is God who works in you to will and to act in order to fulfill his good purpose.*
>
> PHILIPPIANS 2:12 (NIV)

It is our response to God's working in us that Paul encourages the Philippians to embrace. Verse 14 tells us to do so *'without grumbling and arguing'*.

In his letter to the Ephesians, Paul conveys the idea of working out our salvation in line with how God created us in Christ Jesus. We must understand that when God speaks of character, He speaks of Himself. Godly character is light years beyond worldly character.

> *For by grace you have been saved, through faith – and this is not from yourselves, it is the gift of God – not*

by works, so that no one can boast. For we are God's handiwork, created in Christ Jesus to do good works, which God prepared in advance for us to do.

EPHESIANS 2:8-10 (NIV)

The expectations of God to refine our character is not the origin of our salvation but the evidence of it. God's passionate investment in us demands a response. Even in scattered time? Yes, especially in scattered times! What He has prepared for us requires the alignment of our character with His. Thus, adjustments to the Godkind have to be made. His unfolding purpose in us requires stability of our character. This is not self-improvement stuff. This is about allowing the exchange of our sinful nature for His righteous nature to mature in us.

Character refinement was in the works before we were His! God's purpose is intertwined with His ongoing Kingdom dialogue. James' directive is critical to the Kingdom's strategy of spreading the Gospel throughout the entire world. The early believers had to get out of Jerusalem. The go **'Into all the world'** could not be left to convenience. Thus, James writes to those 'sown like seeds among the nations!' In Jesus' parable of the sower, seeds had to be scattered! They had to grow into maturity in environments outside their 'seed packet'! Christianity was a movement before it had a name. Movements move. Seeds have to be scattered. We have to change. We have to grow resolute to the process.

EXPECTATION #2: ABSORPTION OF THE WORD OF GOD

In verse 19 of chapter 1, James says: **'Be quick to listen; but slow to speak. And be slow to become angry, for human anger is never a legitimate tool to promote God's righteous purpose.'** How often do trying times come back to purpose? Anger attracts what's impure and immoral. It equates to character flaws. James offers an alternative to becoming angry.

'Instead, with a sensitive spirit we absorb God's Word which has been implanted within our nature, for the Word of Life has power to continually deliver us.'
JAMES 1:21B

When we absorb the Word of God, the Word of God absorbs our difficulties. He turns our moments of difficulty into blessings! When a sponge absorbs water, the water becomes invisible even though it's still there. In the same way, difficulties may still be present, but they no longer are our focus. The Word of God is.

Hunger for God's Word was planted in us when we received our *born again* nature! Being quick to listen to the Word absorbs our thoughts and expectations so we are delivered from the rabbit trails of anger and anxiety. Listening and listening and listening is the discipline that brings the Word to a point of absorption.

Revelation in His Word radically transforms us. Working out our salvation is the detail work initiated by the Holy Spirit. Absorbing information on any subject requires leaning into it to the point of walking it out. Remember as children leaning as far forward as possible without moving your feet? At some point, we leaned far enough that we had to step forward! Leaning into God's Word until we take a step forward is the same idea. Leaning into God's expectations brings movement. Such leaning should be a vocal part of our daily experience. In tough times, be sure your leaning includes speaking His Word out loud until you take a step forward.

EXPECTATION #3: DOMINION OVER JUDGEMENT

Regardless of how scattered we feel in difficult times, God's mercy must trump condemnation. Tolerance of condemnation breeds more condemnation. Sowing mercy in others, where none has been earned, is a character issue. Because we have required God's mercy in our life, we should never fail to distribute God's mercy to those around us.

> *So we must both speak and act in every respect like those who are destined to be tried by the perfect law of the liberty, and remember that Judgment is merciless for the one who judges others without mercy. So by showing mercy you take dominion over judgement.*
>
> JAMES 2:12-13

Not only should we sow mercy to others but to ourselves, as well. Living above the flood waters of judgment and condemnation defies the status quo of worldly opinion. **Mercy is faith in action.** It takes faith to release mercy where judgement is justified. Faith forward. Cut yourself some slack. Expect God's Word to bear results not because you've been perfect, but because His mercy is perfect.

EXPECTATION #4: SELF-CONTROL

This expectation partners with Expectation #3. James works this principle throughout his letter. Why? Because in trying and troubling times, we are prone to go out of control. Here's what James writes:

> *We all fail in many areas, but especially with our words. Yet if we're able to bridal the words we say we are powerful enough to control ourselves in every way and that means our character is mature and fully developed.*
>
> JAMES 3:2

Through our recycling of disappointment and the words we let fly, we hate this point. It makes us feel like failures. But as with everything else in our lives, God never gives up on us. His expectations remain intact, as should ours.

We know that out of our mouth flows the good, bad, and ugly words of our life. But as James writes in verse 10: '...*this should never be!*' What are your expectations in this area? Until our thought life is tamed, we'll never be able to tame our word life! Proverbs 23:7 (KJV) says **'As a man thinks in his heart, so is he.'** Too often, we fall prey to 'well, I was thinking it, so I may as well say it!' Cliques like this do not foster self-control. In fact, some clichés justify our lack of self-control. Anger loves it!

We have to renew our minds. Remember the word used in the King James version of Proverbs 23:7 – the word 'thinketh' is defined as 'gatekeeper.' We are the gatekeepers of the expectations we think and vocalize in scattered and transitional times. What we allow into our thinking, we give airtime in our speaking. Add doubt and unbelief to those words, and all hell breaks loose.

Bridling our words is powerful and matures our character. Self-control is a discipline that bridles more than our thought life. Raise the gate on your expectations by letting your thoughts fully develop you into Christ's character and expectations. Close the gate on compromising and self-depreciating versions of God's expectations for your life. Wise gatekeepers keep out the wrong thoughts and welcome the healthy ones. Self-control is maintaining a focus on His purpose, so that everything else, our words and actions, line up.

EXPECTATION #5: WISDOM

Wisdom is a partner of revelation. Paul prayed that the Ephesians be filled with the spirit of wisdom and revelation in their knowledge of Jesus. James describes wisdom as:

> *...pure, filled with peace, considerate and teachable, filled with love and never displaying prejudice or hypocrisy, always bearing a beautiful harvest of righteousness. God's seed of wisdom's fruit will be planted with peaceful acts by those who cherish making peace.*
>
> JAMES 3:17-18

Our motivation for seeking Godly wisdom must be based on our desire to be a peacemaker. Nothing else will do. James writes in chapter one:

> *And if anyone longs to be wise, ask God for wisdom and he will give it! He won't see your lack of wisdom as an opportunity to scold you over your failures, but he will overwhelm your failures with his generous grace. Just make sure you ask empowered by confident faith without doubting that you will receive.*
>
> JAMES 1:5-6

Ask for wisdom and mean it. Can you tell when your requests for wisdom are half-hearted? Recognize when you are vacillating in your faith. Vacillating is what I call 'windshield wiper faith' – one minute we believe it, the next we don't - back and forth we go, over and over again. Ever wonder why we can't hear God's answers to our requests? Instability in our faith is a heart condition. Faith up. Have a good talk with yourself. Look yourself in the mirror and get real. Do you want to clarify Expectation #5? Ask! Ask! Ask!

EXPECTATION #6: STANDING FIRM AGAINST THE DEVIL

Be willing to be made low before the Lord and he will exalt you!

JAMES 4:10

A surrendered life to Jesus brings us to a level of servitude that the devil can't understand. The devil has never known surrender to a higher power. But God does. Through Jesus, God knows. We must personalize the line in the King James version: *God resists the proud, but gives grace to the humble.* (I Peter 5:5-6). We must own it. Here are God's intentions behind this principle: God is a lifter. Grace is a lifter. Grace and truth came by Jesus Christ. Everywhere Jesus went, He exuded grace. Grace makes us receptive to faith. If this is new territory for you, John brings us clarity:

> *Moses gave us the Law, but Jesus, the Anointed One, unveils truth wrapped in tender mercy.*
>
> JOHN 1:17

The Apostle Peter clarifies the lifting ability of God.

> *If you bow low in God's awesome presence, he will eventually exalt you as you leave the timing in his hands.*
>
> I PETER 5:6

Everywhere Jesus went, those who humbled themselves were lifted. Think about blind Bartimaeus or the military man with a dying daughter or even Peter on the beach with Jesus after the resurrection. God's a lifter.

In tough times, anxiety typically invades our thoughts. Anxiety is a prideful distraction and totally contrary to humility. Yielding to humility ushers grace onto the stage of our scattered and troubling times. Wherever grace makes an entrance, *lifting* goes into action.

Grace is not a static contributor to our expectations. Grace is like an action hero for all who choose to walk in humility and submission before God. Expectations of God's lifting in our lives should be automatic in a life of faith.

Do you realize how jealous God is for you? Think again about these words: 'passionately invested in you'! James says it this way.

> *Does the scripture mean nothing to you that says, "The Spirit that God breathed into our hearts is a jealous Lover who intensely desires to have more and more of us?" But he continues to pour out more and more grace upon us.*
>
> *For it says, God resists you when you are proud but continually pours out grace when you are humble." So then, surrender to God. Stand up to the devil and resist him and he will turn and run away from you. Move your heart closer and closer to God and he will come even closer to you. But make sure you cleanse your life, you sinners and keep our heart pure and stop doubting.*
> JAMES 4:5-8

James was writing to broken people who were hurt and scattered by persecution. He tells them to come closer. He assures them that God wants to pour out more and more grace on their lives. Our humility before God gives us the fortitude of grace to resist the devil. Our expectations of God's grace should only be based on our humility, not our goodness. Simple? Yes! Our expectation of His grace does not require a complicated theological discussion. Just drop the pride, humble yourself, and receive the grace. Grace is a lifter. His grace will raise your expectations.

EXPECTATION #7: GOD'S RELATIONSHIP BECOMING MORE INTIMATE

The results of the previous 6 expectations is that God comes closer. In scattered times when we are facing nothing but troubling times, God wants to come even closer. It is not God's nature to keep His distance. It is, however, human nature to keep our distance. Why? Because we get angry. We get mad at God. We get mad at ourselves. We get really, really mad. Our expectations get buried when we isolate ourselves from God. But that's a problem we can solve.

God is not limited by our comfort zones in life. He is jealous for us. When we won't move, He moves us. He shakes things up. Until we are separated from all that is familiar, we tend to rely more on all that has been familiar! We hope it never goes away. We want our life to go into reruns, not overturns. We fret and complain. We're shocked. But what if we were passionately invested to the same extent that he is? No complaining. No murmuring. Embracing new expectations. Are your expectations in line with James' letter? Is intimacy with God your number one priority? You need him to come closer. That's going to cost you. But the harvest is worth it. Peacemakers know it.

EXPECTATION #8: EXPECTATION OF HARVEST

Relevant words matter. Reaching our world is complicated. On a recent mission trip to Mexico, one of my interns sat in a coffee shop with a perfect stranger. As she shared her faith with him about Jesus, the stranger had to google 'Jesus' to figure out who she was talking about.

During my time in Canada, the lead pastor often told me of people shaking his hand at the end of a service and telling him that they had never been in a church before! 'Do you mean, not even for a funeral or a wedding?' he asked. Their reply: 'I mean never'! The reality of our relationship with Jesus and the blessings that follow should change our take on all we do, especially in reaching out to a generation that has to google Jesus!

In James 1:25, the apostle writes:

> *But those who set their gaze deeply into the perfecting law of liberty, are fascinated by and respond to the truth they hear and are strengthened by it – they experience God's blessing in all that they do!*

James pushes the envelope further:

> *If you consider yourself to be wise and one who understands the ways of God, advertise it with a beautiful, fruitful life guided by wisdom's gentleness!*
>
> JAMES 3:13

Then, James discusses how Godly wisdom differs from worldly wisdom.

> *But the wisdom from above is always pure, filled with peace, considerate and teachable. It is filled with love and never displays prejudice or hypocrisy in any form and it always bears the beautiful harvest of righteousness! Good seeds of wisdom's fruit will be planted with peaceful acts by those who cherish making peace.*
>
> JAMES 3:17

Harvest in this context is a character and conversation issue. As a character issue, it's about our motives when Godly wisdom is sacrificed on the altar of selfish ambition. As a conversation issue, it points to our interactions in real time with this generation to bring a harvest of souls. James at the end of his letter narrows his narrative to those who have wandered from the truth.

> *Finally, as members of God's beloved family, we must go after the one who wanders from the truth and bring him back. For the one who restores the sinning believer back to God from the error of his way, gives back to his soul life from the dead and covers over countless sins by their demonstration of love!*
>
> JAMES 5:19-20

My point here is that we have to display tangible word play with our world that is relatable. This word play can't be based on a fantasy that all the world is familiar with our Christianese! Relevant words matter to both those who have wandered away from God and those who have never known Him. It takes the Holy Spirit to break down what we know into a vocabulary that transcends cultural and generational differences. The battle is not against those who've never heard; the battle is for them. How we package our demonstration of love for them matters. There are people who slip in and out of our lives each day who need relevant truth from Gods' Word. We can expect opportunity, but we also have to be ready. That's where relevant wisdom comes into play. The Holy Spirit knows how to bring relevant clarity of God's love to those who've never known Him. As Jesus said to his disciples: 'Pray that God will send workers into the harvest.' (KJV)

BEFORE WE GO ON, THINK ABOUT THE FOLLOWING:
Being scattered is normal. Heroes of our faith were often scattered. Think about Abraham, Jacob, Joseph, Moses…need I go on? Being scattered or saddled with difficulties is part of life on planet earth.

- *What are your expectations?*
- *Are your expectations anchored in the Word of God or in your own worldly flirtations?*
- *Are you mastering the need to ask God for wisdom in peaceful times?*
- *Are you prepared?*
- *Are you willing to be matured when life drifts into scattered times?*
- *Is your life surrendered to Jesus Christ?*

Allow me to give the theme of this book a little different twist.

God is passionately invested in building you into someone you could never become without his directions, interventions, and EXPECTATIONS.

I believe, with all my heart, that the best is yet to come. Why? Because God's version of the 'best is yet to come' is Kingdom code for 'going into all the world with the Gospel of Jesus Christ.' That may mean staying where you are geographically. Regardless, it's code for stretching us for His purpose. The ramifications of such, requires the plot twists necessary to refine our character. God's version may very well move us out of our comfort zone. Have you chosen to go there yet?

11

THE GRACE PRINCIPLE

*The will to win is cheap and common, but
the will to train is rare and noble.*
—*Eric Greitens*

GRACE BY DEFINITION

GOD'S DIVINE INFLUENCE ON OUR HEART &
ITS REFELECTION IN THE LIFE.
(Strong's Concordance G5485)

On the road to Damascus, grace hit Saul of Tarsus harder than anything had ever hit him. God's presence knocked him off his horse physically, but it was God's grace that re-charted his life. God confronted Saul's rage and murderous hatred against the first century believers. God saw any attack against His believers as an attack against himself. Thus, in Acts 7:4 (KJV) God confronts Saul: "Saul, Saul, why are you persecuting me?"

Saul had been caught up in the Pharisees' web of religious legalism. Their religious authority and control were threatened by the expansion of believers in Jesus as the Messiah. Their jealousy grew into a raging anger with murderous consequences. Saul had been their number one zealot and hitmaker! Their hatred became his hatred. That hatred was reflected through every fiber of his being. His innocent victims fled for their lives or suffered death.

'Who are you, Lord?' had been Saul's reply to Jesus' question. During the next three days, everything would change. Saul would surrender to Jesus as Lord and Savior. His conversion accelerated the movement of the Christian faith. He became an unstoppable force. Saul, whose name became Paul, lived totally under the influence of God's grace. He lived out the Greek meaning of the word grace. The motivation of his heart spun daily from the influence of God's grace on his heart and its reflection in his life.

It is important to understand that even today, followers of Jesus are seen by Satan as threats. We have an enemy, and he doesn't play fair. He breaks the rules, he distorts the facts, and he ruins lives. He challenges grace's influence on our heart and works to dismiss grace's reflection in our lives. Satan uses people to do his dirty work. His brand of darkness knows no limits. But God's grace is greater. God's influence is greater. His reflection in our lives is powerful.

Here is a story about how Satan tried to use a *good old guy gang* within a legal system to ruin a young lady's life. Notice the quiet influence of grace that eventually changed everything.

INNOCENCE'S STORY
The young lady thought that if she just told the truth, everything would work out. She had never been so wrong. Trumped up charges against her by combative and monstrous self-serving legal experts prevailed.

She was sentenced to 44 years in the state penitentiary. The hateful court system dealt her 21st birthday a deadly blow.

Solitary confinement provided the accommodations of a combo sink/toilet, bed, passthrough slot for meals, and small scenic widow to the outside prison air! From her privileged and Christian upbringing, she was now in solitary hell. Her innocence had no voice. Angered for months at the unfair turn her life had taken, she eventually escaped into the only reading material provided her, the Bible. She read it through and through. Her favorite texts were from the Old Testament stories. In them, she read of God's vindication against evil, and she waited to be vindicated.

Toward the end of her first year, she decided to find a way to make the most of it. If this was to be her life, she thought, what could she do? She had to find a starting place. Smile! Yes, she could smile. She could even say 'good morning,' until it seemed real. This was a turning point. Her new identity would be more characterized by her helpful countenance and generous spirit than by the clothes she wore and the world in which she lived. Grace walked in!

Within limited opportunities, she found opportunity. In the testing of a lifetime, she found a life. In the boisterous and profane dialogue behind prison walls, she listened to the conversation in her heart. She lived the wisdom gained from her Christian upbringing. Key to it all, she reached out whenever possible to meet the needs of others. Her expectations of exoneration became her default mindset. God's grace created a new familiar in the times that had scattered her. Taking advantage of her opportunity to live peacefully within a flawed system changed her.

Eleven years later she was exonerated. Several of those within the corrupt legal system had died. With their hateful arrogance gone, God's grace triumphed. At the age of 32, she walked free, her record purged. Her character exonerated. Today she works as a trained nurse, adding value to the community where she was raised.

This story is true on all accounts. It goes to show that even in the most extreme cases, God's grace is transformative. It was the grace of God that softened the hard edge of unfairness to survive life behind bars as an innocent.

Remember, how we see ourselves matters. We can't consistently live in a way contrary to how we see ourselves. In transitions, two things are true:

1. It is self-destructive to think that everything is up to us. It is self-limiting to think that it all depends on our willpower and our expertise.
2. If we see ourselves as 'king of the heap,' we cut ourselves short of God's grace.

Stubborn egos become our stumbling blocks. We may go through the motions of a transition by implementing the same systems and skill sets we've always used. We may call on the same people for help that we have always called. We may survive an unfair transition, even do it well. But afterwards we live a compromised lifestyle. When we do, we look ourselves in the mirror and see only a lesser person than the one God created. God created us to live beyond average, beyond normal and beyond a limited version of ourselves. Grace makes the difference. To be the intended reflection of God's grace, we cannot *perform*! We need to draw from a source that is unlimited. Willpower is limited. It will fail us, but grace will empower us.

WILL POWER VS GRACE POWER

What's the difference between our will power and God's Grace power?

Great question. We know that grace is the critical force that made our salvation possible. Salvation is an eternal life experience!

> *For if you publicly declare with your mouth that Jesus is Lord and believe in your heart that God raised him from the dead, <u>you will experience salvation</u>. The heart that believes in him receives the gift of the righteousness of God – and then the mouth confesses, resulting in salvation.*
>
> ROMANS 10:9B-10

Notice that faith must be in two places: our heart and our mouth. So must His grace. Our will power is not mentioned. The experience is about His grace power. Paul's writing to the Christians in Rome proves this ongoing experience. Faith certainly did not end at salvation, and neither does grace nor peace. Paul writes:

> *May His joyous grace and total wellbeing, flowing from our Father and the Lord Jesus Christ rest upon you.*
>
> ROMANS 1:1B

> *The promise depends on faith so that it can be experienced as a grace gift.*
>
> ROMANS 4:16

> *Now we are held in the grip of grace.*
>
> ROMANS 5:17

Grace is not just saving grace. God's grace is living grace. Grace is a gift that keeps on giving and takes us beyond our needs. Grace is expansive for the benefit of others.

God's marvelous grace imparts to each one of us varying gifts and ministries that are uniquely ours. Thrive in your grace gift.

ROMANS 12:6

Paul learned what it was to be 'graced.' He knew where his will power was limited and where grace took up the slack. In II Corinthians 12:9, he shares with the Corinthian church how he discovered grace's enabling power. In this test, Paul admits that his willpower wasn't enough. He learned that in all situations, especially those beyond his skillsets and willpower, God's grace is sufficient.

The word 'sufficiency' in the King James version of II Corinthians 12:9 comes from a word meaning 'to lift, to raise (the voice), to weigh anchor.' In II Corinthians 9:8, a different word is translated as sufficiency. This word means 'to arrive competent as if coming into season'!

When we lean into these truths, a path appears. From within us, God's grace makes us competent to arrive in any season with the sufficiency needed. He even promises that there is a grace for giving that will overwhelm us!

Yes, God is more than ready to overwhelm you with every form of grace, so that you will have more than enough of everything – every moment and in every way.

II CORINTHIANS 9:8

Regardless of our situation, there is enough grace to be multiplied as needed.

May God's delightful grace and peace be cascaded over you many times over.

I PETER 1:2B

When Paul discovered that the grace of God was sufficient, he also discovered that grace is unlimited, expandable, multifaceted, gift-heavy, and tough all wrapped up in one. Grace is strengthening not because we deserve it, but because God prefers it. Paul cautions believers in II Corinthians 6:2 not to let the grace of God lose its effect. That means we are expected to live under the effect of grace.

God's grace in our lives equips us to live self-controlled:

> *God's marvelous grace has manifested in person, bringing salvation for everyone. This same grace teaches us how to live each day as we turn our backs on ungodliness and indulgent lifestyles, and it equips us to live self-controlled, upright, Godly lives in this present age.*
>
> TITUS 2:11-12

Consider the truths behind the following scriptures on God's grace:

> *He gave us resurrection life and drew us to himself by his holy calling on our life. And it wasn't because of any good we have done, but because of his divine pleasure and marvelous grace that confirmed our union with the anointed Jesus, even before time began!*
>
> II TIM 1:9

> *When the meeting had finally broken up, many of those in attendance, both Jews and converts to Judaism, tagged along with Paul and Barnabas, who continued to persuade them to go deeper in their understanding of God's Grace.*
>
> ACTS 13:43

Paul's life is living proof of the power of grace exercised consistently in a life full of challenging transitions. God empowered him to creatively expand the Gospel throughout the known world. Grace encouraged the young church through letters Paul wrote from prison. When the world tried to shut Paul down, he found sufficient grace to lift him up.

MAXIMIZING GRACE

Grace moves the dial on our capacity and brings us to a level of toughness in transitions. We don't have to live limited by our will-power! This is the message James writes as well to those scattered by persecution. It is the message of martyrs and novices, alike.

Finishing what God has started in our life is expanded through God's grace. Paul writes the Romans Christians:

> *...Even in times of trouble we have a joyful confidence knowing that our pressures will develop in us patient endurance. And patient endurance will refine our char-acter, and proven character leads us back to hope. And this hope is not a disappointing fantasy, because we can now experience the endless love of God cascading into our hearts through the Holy Spirit who lives in us.*
> ROMANS 5:3-5

Transitions are proving grounds for God's Grace to operate at full throttle in our lives. The strengthening power of grace moves us into dimensions of life unprecedented by mere willpower.

FALLING FROM GRACE

Paul in his letter to the church in Galatia warned of what he called 'falling from grace.' His point was that if we go back to trying to earn our righteousness by doing works, we are no longer living in the grace of God. This point needs to be clear to all believers. James tells us that there will be times when we seem to be facing nothing but difficulties. When that happens, he says, we must realize that our faith is being tested. He doesn't say that we are losing our salvation, although if we are led by our feelings, we may think so.

We may think that God is disappointed in us, and we're about to lose salvation. Then Satan pounces on us with condemnation and points out our imperfections. He suggests that we need to do some kind of self-inflected penitence. Everything spirals downward from there. Suddenly our focus rebounds to earning salvation through works. We try being really, really good, but we're not good at it. Feelings come and go in every direction, but grace does not. It's there for us!

In the context of Paul's writing to the Galatians, he has found that Jewish zealots had perverted the salvation message. In fact, they polluted grace by blending the Gospel with strict Old Covenant practices. Prominent in this blend was the requirement that all men be circumcised. Not a popular practice among the newly converted Gentile male population. Adhering to the Old Covenant was impossible because the law is limited by the weakness of our human nature. (Romans 8:3)

Works + grace = Disaster. Why? Because measuring up leads to more and more measures. It becomes a never-ending list. Paul did not intend the phrase 'falling from grace' to mean losing our salvation. Paul is crystal clear. Consider these verses.

> *I, Paul, tell you: If you think there is benefit in circumcision and Jewish regulations, then you're acting as though Jesus the Anointed One is not enough.*
>
> GALATIANS 5:2

If you want to be made holy by fulfilling the obligations of the law, you have cut off more than your flesh – you have cut yourselves off from the Anointed One and have fallen away from the revelation of grace.

GALATIANS 5:4

Throughout church history, salvation by works is a culprit that raises its ugly head to draw believers backward. But shouldn't we still do works? Yes, but not to earn our salvation. Faith works in us and through us because we are already saved. Faith produces works to glorify God, not to impress Him.

Paul challenged the Ephesians to '**Therefore be imitators of God, as beloved children.**' Ephesians 5:1 (ESV) Children who feel loved have an expansive vigor and zeal. As those loved by God and empowered with grace for every situation and transition, we must never lose grip on this fact. We are loved by God. Dearly loved children don't run from their parents when they have a problem. They run to their parents. Dearly loved children of God do the same. We run to Him not away from Him. Everything accomplished through Jesus is ours as a gift. As new creations in Christ, we are new, fresh, whole, empowered, and graced for whatever comes at us. Every opportunity comes with access to the overwhelming love and grace of God. Paul learned that he could do all things through Christ. He had to practice a life of grace based on who he was in Christ Jesus.

The will to win is cheap and common, but the will to train is rare and noble.

ERIC GREITENS

It is uncommon in our world for people to fulfill their potential in the midst of transitions. Only grace can make a difference. Training ourselves to walk in grace every day is critical before, during, and after every transition. Grace gives us the power to stand tough in the crosshairs of difficulties and opportunities.

LET ME ASK YOU A FEW MORE QUESTIONS:

- How frequently do you draw away from the grace of God in your daily life?
- Are you part-time or full-time in the walk of grace as God intended?
- Do you take time to reflect on the wonder of His grace working through you?
- Are you committed to making grace-adjustments rather than work-adjustments when you fail?

ACCESSING THIS GRACE

To get the most out of scattered and trying times we need God's unlimited power. That's the power of **GRACE. Grace isn't an earned quality or skillset. Grace is a gift. It is unlimited.** Leveraging grace affects all the other chapters. They intermingle.

Life without Grace? Whether we live with a *poor me attitude* or a *I've got this* attitude, we limit grace and our *opportunities.* We may pass *the test of the transition,* but without grace, it will leave us hollow. We may *listen quickly,* yet without grace, we hear incompletely. We may meet its challenge, but without grace, will fail to pull in *wisdom* beyond our past experiences. If we see ourselves too busy to *reach out* and help someone else, we will finish in a weak second place to the Grace God extends. *Expectations* that focus only on the survival mode miss the intended mark and measure of grace. Please notice how the absence of grace affects everything.

Hebrews 4:16 tells us to come boldly to the Throne of Grace. Why? To obtain mercy and find grace to help in the time of need. What are times of need? Every day. Every day, we need His mercy and grace. Grace is all encompassing. Grace partners in scripture with peace, faith, truth, and so much more. The Gospel is the Good News of God's overwhelming grace and truth.

> *So now we come freely and boldly to where love is enthroned, to receive mercy's kiss and discover the grace we urgently need to strengthen us in our times of weakness.*
> HEBREWS 4:16

GRACE WILL:

- **Open your eyes to see the opportunities hiding in plain sight.**
- **Toughen and strengthen you to rejoice when your faith is tested.**
- **Sharpen your listening skills to God's presence when life gets noisy.**
- **Discern between Godly wisdom and what's trending in society's fault-line.**
- **Release mercy through us to keep us outwardly focused.**
- **Renew our expectations on God's Word rather than the world's street smarts.**
- **Release God's divine influence into our life in sync with his Kingdom's narrative.**

Always know that in scattered times –

**GOD IS PASSIONATELY INVESTED
IN YOU BECOMING SOMEONE YOU
COULD NEVER BE WITHOUT HIS
DIRECTION AND INTERVENTION.**

CONCLUSION

We have now explored the 7 principles found in James' letter. Let's conclude by focusing on the dramatic story in Mark 9:14-24 and the need to be consistent in our faith.

Jesus, along with Peter, James and John, came walking down the mountain of transfiguration. They were met with a large group of people arguing with the other nine disciples. Jesus asked what they were arguing about.

A man in the crowd spoke up and told Jesus that he had a son possessed by a demon, making him mute. The devil would throw the boy into convulsions, making him roll around foaming at the mouth. Sometimes the demon even threw the boy into the fire. The man brought his son to the disciples hoping they could deliver him, but the disciples weren't strong enough.

Jesus' initial response surprised the crowd. He confronted the crowd, saying, "Why are you such a faithless people? How much longer must I remain with you and put up with your unbelief?" (Mark 9:19)

In scattered times, we need to confront ourselves with a similar question, not to condemn but to awaken us. We must listen to the words we hear ourselves saying in such times.

Too often we elaborate on the details of our situation as if verbalizing them will bring us hope. It won't. Hope comes from hearing and believing the Word of God.

Our decision to be led by the Holy Spirit changes everything. His presence is evidence of God's passionate investment in our life. If this is a new thought, please read Romans 8:1-6. When we meditate in this scripture, we begin to realize that the Holy Spirit really lives in our born again spirit.

We are no longer limited to what our intellect and emotions dictate. Their narrative is inferior to God's narrative in His Word. As we begin to speak the Word over our unfamiliar times, our faith will thrive. Slowly, we begin to see our situation from God's perspective. His wisdom will change and update the worldview of our circumstances.

Let's return to the story in Mark 9. The father of the demon-possessed son said to Jesus something like this: "If you can do anything to help my son, please feel sorry enough for us to do something."

Jesus replied, "What do you mean *if?* If you are able to believe, all things are possible to the believer" (Mark 9:23)!

The father responded, "I do believe, Lord; help my little faith" (Mark 9:24).

Here's my point. Our faith grows in the Word of God just as the father's faith that day grew upon hearing Jesus' words. But remember that a little faith is all we need if our little faith is consistent. The father's faith in this story was inconsistent.

With faith, we can walk through unfamiliar times even when we feel a little scattered. Even when we don't have all the answers, we can know God's grace in its fullness. We can learn to lean into His Word for wisdom. God freely gives us wisdom. He will rebuild our expectations on His Word. We need to calm down and really listen. Making these course corrections in our heart and mind empowers us to become more outward focused. As we do, we will come to expect and see opportunities in the midst of what's testing us. I've had to learn to fine tune my listening to God's reality rather than settle on how I feel. I've had to stop replaying the circumstances of what's scattering me and instead, start rehearsing the Word of God.

Finally, it is important to see ourselves as the traveler not the tourist. We must guard against buying into someone else's experience. Traveling with expectancy based on our relationship with Jesus Christ and the Holy Spirit is a game changer. So is allowing the Holy Spirit to father us through challenging moments.

What if we leverage God's Word against what's scattering us? What if we lean into the strengths of our bias until we see opportunities that will grow our faith even stronger. Then we will know the power of God rising up inside of us as we rejoice in Him. He will share His wisdom because He wants to. No more will we fall into the mindset of saying *if* God is able or *if* God wants to.

IF YOU BELIEVE THAT ALL THINGS ARE POSSIBLE WITH GOD, I GUARANTEE TO YOU THE FOLLOWING:

- You will see invaluable opportunity in your tough times.
- You will maneuver through what's testing your faith by God's Word.

- You will fine tune your listening until you live in sync with what He's authoring in your life.
- You will draw practical day-to-day wisdom from God's wisdom as He invests in your life.
- You will live outwardly focused even when feeling inward insanity.
- You will build life changing expectations in the fog of the in-between places of your transition.
- You will reflect God's grace in your life as it influences your heart.

Always remember:

**GOD IS PASSIONATELY INVESTED
IN YOU BECOMING SOMEONE YOU
COULD NEVER BE WITHOUT HIS
DIRECTION AND INTERVENTION.**

I hope the book encouraged and challenged you. Don't forget to download your free 21 Day Scattered Times Devotional at my website:

Genebracknow.com

Self-Publishing School

NOW IT'S YOUR TURN

Discover the EXACT 3-step blueprint you need
to become a bestselling author in 3 months.

Self-Publishing School helped me, and now I want
them to help you with this FREE WEBINAR!

Even if you're busy, bad at writing, or
don't know where to start, you CAN write
a bestseller and build your best life.

With tools and experience across a variety
of niches and professions, Self-Publishing
School is the only resource you need to
take your book to the finish line!

Watch this FREE WEBINAR now, and
Say "YES" to becoming a bestseller:

https://self-publishingschool.com/
Click on "Join Our Free Training"

ABOUT THE AUTHOR

Gene Brack has lived a life focused on faith and education. For more than 50 years, he has ministered the message of the Good News through faith in Jesus Christ. Gene holds both a BA and an , MFA in theatre from William Carey University and the University of Southern Mississippi, respectively.

He has pastored in the creative arts as well as serving in various church positions, including Pastor and Associate Pastor. He is known as a gifted teacher of the Word of God in Mississippi, Alabama, Iowa, and Illinois. He served as Dean of Victory Bible College at MyVictory Church in Lethbridge, Alberta. In addition to ministry, he also served as Academic Dean and instructor with Hamilton Technical College in Davenport, Iowa.

Thank You for Reading My Book!

I am available to minister the truths in this book and serve churches in any way that would be valuable to them. You may contact me at gene@genebracknow.com or my website genebracknow.com

Please leave me an honest review on Amazon and let me know what you gained from this book.

Thanks so much!

Gene

Made in the USA
Columbia, SC
21 June 2020